AQA German

AS

Grammar
Workbook

David Riddell

OXFORD

UNIVERSITY PRESS

Great Clarendon Street, Oxford, OX2 6DP, United Kingdom

Oxford University Press is a department of the University of Oxford.
It furthers the University's objective of excellence in research, scholarship,
and education by publishing worldwide. Oxford is a registered trade mark of
Oxford University Press in the UK and in certain other countries

Text © David Riddell 2013
Original illustrations © Oxford University Press 2014

The moral rights of the authors have been asserted

First published by Nelson Thornes Ltd in 2013
This edition published by Oxford University Press in 2014

British Library Cataloguing in Publication Data
Data available

978-1-4085-2012-3

12

Printed in Spain

Acknowledgements

Cover photograph: iStockphoto/Ralf Hetler
Illustrations: Andy Keylock
Page make-up: Hart McLeod Ltd, Cambridge

Contents

How to use this book

Transition

The activities and guidance here are to help you bridge the gap between GCSE and AS. There may be particular areas where you are still not confident or where you wish to revise. Look through this at the start of your course and decide what you need to practise. You can always refer back later in the year.

Order of topics

This book is divided into four sections, each of which corresponds to a topic in the AQA German AS course. While practice activities use simple vocabulary from various subject areas, grammar points are covered in the same order as in the Student Book. This is to help you practise as you go along, reinforcing what you have learned in the classroom with further activities at home.

Mixed practice

At the end of each section there are some mixed practice activities covering the different points you have encountered. You can try these throughout the year or use them for revision while you prepare for your listening, reading and writing exam.

Test yourself

These activities follow a format you are more likely to encounter in the listening, reading and writing paper – hence the rubrics are in German. When you are in the exam you will not be told which grammar points you need to practise, or that a question is particularly geared towards testing your grammar knowledge and accuracy. Therefore it is important to get used to tackling this type of question with confidence.

Longer activities

Some activities will require more extended responses or offer the opportunity for more creative work. For these it will be suggested that you work on a separate sheet of paper. Alternatively you can type up and save your answers to refer to again when revising.

Receptive knowledge only

The AQA specification, which you can consult online, includes a list of the grammatical structures you will be expected to have studied. Some structures are marked with an (R), which indicates receptive knowledge only is required. This means you need to understand phrases and sentences which use the structures but will not need to apply them in your own written and spoken work. Even so, if you are confident in using them yourself you should do so!

Grammatik

These offer extra support in understanding the point being tested. Don't refer to them unless you need to! If you need additional information, go to the grammar reference section of your Student Book.

Tipp

These offer extra 'handy hints' for tackling different questions, remembering particular rules and applying your grammar knowledge in practice.

1 Replace the underlined nouns with the correct subject pronouns. Write them in the brackets.

a Der Junge (_er_) spielt gern Tennis.

b Die Leute (_Sie_) waren sehr freundlich.

c Die Tasche (_sie_) ist leer.

d Das Buch (_es_) ist auf dem Tisch.

e Mein Onkel und meine Tante (_sie_) kommen morgen zu Besuch.

f Der Kuli (_er_) ist in meiner Tasche.

g Wo sind meine Ohrringe (_sie_)?

Grammatik

Object pronouns can be used for the direct object (**accusative**) or the indirect object (**dative**). They are as follows:

subject (nominative)	direct object (accusative)		indirect object (dative)	
ich	mich	me	mir	to/for me
du	dich	you	dir	to/for you
er	ihn	him/it	ihm	to/for him/it
sie	sie	her/it	ihr	to/for her/it
es	es	it	ihm	to/for it
wir	uns	us	uns	to/for us
ihr	euch	you	euch	to/for you
Sie	Sie	you	Ihnen	to/for you
sie	sie	them	ihnen	to/for them

Grammatik

Personal pronouns are used instead of nouns to avoid mentioning the same person or thing again. Like nouns, they can be used in different cases (but the genitive is not in common use).

Subject pronouns (**nominative**) are as follows:

ich	I
du	you (familiar, singular)
er/sie/es	he/she/it
wir	we
ihr	you (familiar, plural)
Sie	you (polite, sing./pl.)
sie	they

Tipp

Make a point of learning the personal pronouns in each case as soon as you can. For example, you could learn them in threes:

ich–mich–mir, du–dich–dir, and so on.

2 Underline the nominative pronouns, circle the accusative pronouns and place a tick above the dative pronouns in each of the sentences. Then translate the sentences into English.

a Sie hat mir einen Bleistift geliehen.

_____

b Hast du ihr die Karte geschickt?

_____

c Er hat es ihnen gegeben.

_____

d Habt ihr es uns nicht gebracht?

_____

e Sie hat ihm ein Foto versprochen.

_____

Tipp

How to say 'it'

Be careful when using the word 'it' because you must choose the correct word depending on case and gender.

Ich habe einen Kuli. **Er** ist blau. (nominative, masculine)

Ich habe keinen Bleistift. Ich habe **ihn** verloren. (accusative, masculine)

3 Complete the sentences with the correct pronouns. Check the cases very carefully.

a _Sie_ haben _____ die Geschenke gegeben. (_They, to them_)

b _____ besucht _____ am Freitag. (_She, him_)

c _____ findet _____ lustig. (_He, it_ [neuter])

d _____ haben _____ das Auto verkauft. (_We, him_)

e _____ hat _____ gestern gesehen. (_She, you_ [fam. sg.])

f _____ habt _____ _____ letzte Woche geschickt. (_You_ [fam. pl.], _it_ [neuter], _to him_)

g _____ habe _____ das Buch gegeben. (_I, you_ [pol.])

h _____ schickt _____ eine SMS. (_He, me_)

1 Place a tick beside the verbs which have correct endings, and correct the others.

a er kaufst ☐   d wir spielen ☐   g du glaube ☐

b Sie lernen ☐   e sie wohnt ☐   h wir trennen ☐

c ich kochst ☐   f ich machen ☐   i ihr sucht ☐

2 Write in the present tense form of the infinitive given in brackets.

a Mein Bruder _____ einen Samstagsjob. (**suchen**)

b Seit 10 Jahren _____ wir an der Küste. (**wohnen**)

c Am Samstag _____ ich eine neue Hose. (**kaufen**)

d Er _____ jeden Morgen auf den Bus. (**warten**)

e Die Kinder _____ Englisch und Französisch in der Schule. (**lernen**)

f Was _____ du nach der Schule? (**machen**)

g Johannes und Steffi, _____ ihr den Müll? (**trennen**)

h Das Konzert _____ um 22.30 Uhr. (**enden**)

3 Find in the grid 10 strong verbs (in their *du* or *er/sie/es* forms only). Words can be read in **every** direction. All the verbs used appear on this page, but not necessarily in the same form.

u	t	h	c	i	r	p	s	l
t	b	t	n	s	k	c	l	i
w	r	b	i	z	h	g	r	e
ä	i	h	s	l	q	i	n	s
s	t	g	ä	r	t	b	u	t
c	s	f	n	f	g	s	v	q
h	s	i	e	h	s	t	v	z
t	f	l	i	h	z	k	g	s

_____

_____

_____

_____

_____

_____

_____

_____

_____

_____

4 Translate these phrases containing strong verbs into German. Refer to a list of strong verbs to help you.

a he speaks _____

b we are reading _____

c you (*fam. sing.*) help _____

d I see _____

e she gives _____

f you (*fam. pl.*) recommend _____

g she steals _____

h they are sleeping _____

Grammatik

The **present tense** is used to describe something happening now or something which happens regularly:

I am doing homework. **I do** homework every day.

Both of these sentences just use the present tense in German:

*Ich **mache** gerade Hausaufgaben.*
*Ich **mache** jeden Tag Hausaufgaben.*

Regular (also called **weak**) verbs form the present tense following the same pattern. Take the infinitive and knock off the ending -*en* (or just -*n* if there is no e) to leave the **stem**:

machen → mach-
plaudern → plauder-

Add the correct ending to the stem, depending on who or what is doing the action of the verb:

ich mache
du machst
er/sie/es macht
wir machen
ihr macht
Sie/sie machen

If the stem ends in *d* or *t*, the letter e must be added before the present tense verb ending -*st* and -*t*:

finden → find- → du findest
antworten → antwort- → er antwortet

Grammatik

Irregular (also called **strong**) verbs form the present tense using the same endings as weak verbs, but there is usually a vowel change in the *du* and *er/sie/es* forms (see verb tables from page 66 onwards).

fahren → ich fahre BUT *du fährst, er/sie/es fährt, wir fahren*

Other verbs which change the same way are: *fallen, schlafen, tragen, waschen*.

geben → ich gebe BUT *du gibst, er/sie/es gibt, wir geben*

Likewise: *essen, helfen, nehmen (nimmst), sprechen, sterben*.

sehen → ich sehe BUT *du siehst, er/sie/es sieht, wir sehen*

Likewise: *lesen, empfehlen, stehlen*.

Grammatik

Reflexive verbs are more common in German than in English. They can be weak or strong and are formed in the normal way. However, they are used with a reflexive pronoun which usually follows the verb:

*ich wasche **mich*** — I wash myself

*du wäschst **dich*** — you wash yourself, etc.

1 Complete the sentences with the correct form of *haben* or *sein*.

a Ich _____ meiner Freundin eine E-Mail geschickt.

b Meine Mutter _____ über eine Urlaubsreise im Internet gelesen.

c Die Werbung _____ heutzutage sehr wichtig geworden.

d Vom Zug _____ wir den Kölner Dom gesehen.

e Was _____ ihr gestern Abend gemacht?

f Ich _____ zehn Tage in einem Luxushotel geblieben.

g Mein Bruder _____ schon nach Hause gegangen.

h Nach dem Frühstück _____ ihr Vater das Auto gewaschen.

i _____ du ein neues Handy gekauft?

j Im Mai _____ meine Freunde und ich nach Genf geflogen.

2 Complete the sentences with the past participle of the verb in brackets. Remember to check whether the verb is regular (weak) or irregular (strong). Then translate the sentences into English.

a Wir haben Fotos von der Hochzeit _____ . **(machen)**

_____

b Der Junge hat sich den Arm _____ . **(brechen)**

_____

c Ich habe diese Fernsehsendung langweilig _____ . **(finden)**

_____

d Wir sind gestern in die Stadtmitte _____ . **(fahren)**

_____

e Sie hat ihrer Schwester mit den Hausaufgaben _____ . **(helfen)**

_____

3 Complete these sentences in German. Use the verbs in the box below.

a Ich _____ den Film _____ . (*have seen*)

b Er _____ meine E-Mail _____ . (*received*)

c Wir _____ in diesem Hotel _____ . (*have stayed*)

d Meine Mutter _____ einkaufen _____ . (*went*)

e _____ du das Geld _____ ? (*Have found*)

f Die Kinder _____ Fußball im Park _____ . (*played*)

> gehen   bleiben   sehen   spielen   finden   erhalten

Grammatik

The perfect tense describes events in the past. To form it, you need the correct form of the auxiliary **verb** (*haben* or *sein*) and the **past participle** at the end of the sentence or clause.

*Ich **habe** einen MP3-Spieler **gekauft**.*
I (have) bought an MP3-player.

*Ich **bin** nach Hause **gegangen**.*
I went home.

Use *haben* with most verbs, including reflexive verbs:

*Ich **habe** mich geduscht.* I (have) showered.

Use *sein* with verbs involving **motion** or a **change of state**:

*Ich **bin** geschwommen.* I swam/have swum.

*Er **ist** eingeschlafen.* He fell/has fallen asleep.

Use *sein* with *bleiben* (to stay), *werden* (to become) and *sein* (to be):

*wir **sind** geblieben* we (have) stayed

*ich **bin** geworden* I became/have become

*er **ist** gewesen* he has been

Forming the past participle

For **weak** (regular) verbs, take the -en off the infinitive (or just -n if there is no e) to leave the **stem**. Now add *ge-* at the beginning and -t at the end:

*spielen → spiel → **gespielt***

*wandern → wander → **gewandert***

For **strong** (irregular) verbs, you should learn the past participles as you go along, including these:

*gehen → **gegangen***
*kommen → **gekommen***
*schwimmen → **geschwommen***
*sprechen → **gesprochen***

Tipp

The past participles of inseparable verbs (weak and strong) such as **be**suchen (to visit) and **ver**sprechen (to promise) look the same as the basic verbs' past participles, but without *ge-*:

*suchen → ich habe ge**sucht***
*besuchen → ich habe be**sucht***
*sprechen → wir haben ge**sprochen***
*versprechen → wir haben ver**sprochen***

1 Read the sentences and fill in the gaps with the correct imperfect form of *haben* or *sein* so that they make sense.

a Gestern _____ Sonntag und ich _____ keine Schule.

b Nach der Reise _____ wir sehr müde.

c Die Mädchen _____ traurig, denn sie _____ kein Geld für das Konzert.

d Wo _____ du am Wochenende?

e Ich _____ einfach keine Zeit zum Trainieren.

f Er _____ ganz froh, weil er Geburtstag _____.

2 Choose the correct word to complete these sentences in the imperfect tense.

a Wir **wollen / wollten / wollte** am Samstag den neuen Film sehen.

b Mein Vater **musste / mussten / muss** das Auto reparieren.

c Nach der Disco **soll /sollte / solltest** Andrea gleich nach Hause gehen.

d Weil die Jugendlichen zu jung waren, **durften / dürfen / durfte** sie keinen Alkohol trinken.

e Mein Freund und ich **konnte / können / konnten** die Hausaufgaben nicht machen.

3 Memorise the imperfect verb forms in the grammar boxes. Then try to complete these sentences using the imperfect form of the verb given in brackets without looking anything up.

a Marcus _____ am Wochenende zelten gehen. (**wollen**)

b Leider _____ ich meinen Fotoapparat nicht finden. (**können**)

c Jan und sein Bruder _____ sofort mit dem Schuldirektor sprechen. (**müssen**)

d In der Schule _____ die Schülerinnen keine großen Ohrringe tragen. (**dürfen**)

e Was _____ ich machen? (**sollen**)

f Um fit zu bleiben, _____ Karla jeden Tag 10 Kilometer laufen. (**müssen**)

g _____ dein jüngerer Bruder mitkommen? (**dürfen**)

h Zum Glück _____ er die Karten im Internet bestellen. (**können**)

Grammatik

The **imperfect tense** (also known as the simple past) tends to be used more in written German, but can also be used in speech. You will have encountered it with the irregular verbs *sein* (*ich war* – I was), *haben* (*ich hatte* – I had) and *geben* (*es gab* – there was/were).

ich war	*ich hatte*
du warst	*du hattest*
er/sie/es war	*er/sie/es hatte*
wir waren	*wir hatten*
ihr wart	*ihr hattet*
Sie/sie waren	*Sie/sie hatten*

Grammatik

You will have also come across the imperfect tense with modal verbs:

können → *ich konnte* (I could, was able to)

wollen → *ich wollte* (I wanted to)

müssen → *ich musste* (I had to)

dürfen → *ich durfte* (I was allowed to)

and possibly:

mögen → *ich mochte* (I liked to)

sollen → *ich sollte* (I was supposed to)

All of these verbs add the same endings as the imperfect tense of *haben*.

Tipp

Be very careful to notice when a vowel has an umlaut. For instance, here all the imperfect forms of modal verbs do not have it! The addition of an umlaut changes the meaning: compare *ich mochte* (I liked) with *ich möchte* (I would like).

Grammatik

Cases are used in German to show how the different words in a sentence work together to make sense. German has four cases: **nominative, accusative, genitive** and **dative**. We see them in certain words such as the definite article ('the'), the indefinite article ('a'), pronouns (see page 5), possessive adjectives (see pages 32 and 53) etc.

Nominative

The subject of a sentence is the person or thing doing the action of the verb and it is shown by the **nominative** case, e.g.

The **woman** has a son. **I** have read the novel.

Accusative

The direct object of a sentence is the person or thing having the action of the verb done to it and it is shown by the **accusative** case, e.g.

The woman has **a son**. I have read **the novel**.

To say the above sentences in German, we need to know how the definite and indefinite articles change depending on the case used. They also change according to the gender and number (singular/plural) of the noun.

	definite article ('the')				indefinite article ('a')			kein ('not a', 'no')			
	masc.	fem.	neut.	plural	masc.	fem.	neut.	masc.	fem.	neut.	plural
nom.	der	die	das	die	ein	eine	ein	kein	keine	kein	keine
acc.	den	die	das	die	einen	eine	ein	keinen	keine	kein	keine

1 Underline the nominative and circle the accusative in each of these sentences.

a Das Mädchen hat heute den Schlüssel verloren.

b Der Lehrer hat einen Volkswagen.

c Am Wochenende muss der Mann den Rasen mähen.

d In der Pause essen meine Freunde und ich einen Schokoriegel oder eine Banane.

e Mit ihrem Sohn hat sie überhaupt keine Geduld.

f Die Schülerin hat keinen Kuli und kein Heft.

g Den Hund habe ich nicht gesehen.

h Gestern hat ein Junge einen Zwanzigeuroschein im Park gefunden.

i Der Mann und die Frau haben das Haus gekauft.

j Die Dame kennt der Mann nicht.

2 Complete the sentences with the correct endings where necessary. Make sure that you check the gender and number of the nouns, shown as m/f/n/pl.

a D__ Junge (m) hat ein__ Portemonnaie (n) gefunden.

b Ich habe ein__ Meerschweinchen (n) und ein__ Katze (f), aber kein__ Goldfisch (m).

c Am Donnerstag besichtigen wir d__ Fernsehturm (m).

d D__ Kinder (pl) haben d__ Film (m) schon gesehen.

e In der Zukunft möchte ich ein__ Haus (n) auf dem Land.

f D__ Mädchen (n) hat mir ein__ Geburtstagskarte (f) geschickt.

g Gestern hat sie kein__ E-Mails (pl) bekommen.

h D__ Mann (m) kenne ich gar nicht.

Grammatik

Note that in the accusative case, only the masculine forms differ from the nominative. Also the indefinite article doesn't have a plural form.

We can now translate the English sentences above into German:

nom.   acc.
Die Frau hat **einen Sohn.**

nom.   acc.
Ich habe **den Roman** gelesen.

Note that the word *kein* uses the same case endings as the indefinite article:

*Er hat **einen** Hund.* He has a dog.

*Er hat **keinen** Hund.* He doesn't have a dog.

To form the plural in the nominative and accusative, use *keine* (not any, no):

*Ich habe **keine** Äpfel gekauft.* I didn't buy any apples/I bought no apples.

1 Underline the words in the dative case in each sentence.

a Die Lehrerin hat dem Kind einen Kuli gegeben.

b Er wollte den Obdachlosen kein Geld geben.

c Die Kundin hat dem Hotelleiter einen Brief geschrieben.

d Ich habe einer Freundin eine E-Mail geschickt.

2 Underline the direct objects and circle the indirect objects in each sentence. Then translate the sentences into English.

a Ich habe der Lehrerin die Fotos gezeigt.

_____

b Der Mann im Verkehrsamt hat der Familie ein preiswertes Hotel empfohlen.

_____

c Mein Bruder hat einem Freund einen alten Tennisschläger geliehen.

_____

d Dem Chef habe ich kein Wort gesagt.

_____

e Die Ärztin hat einem Mann die Tabletten verschrieben.

_____

3 Choose the correct option for the direct and indirect object. Then translate the sentences into English.

a Unsere Lehrerin hat **die / der** Klasse **eine / einer** Geschichte vorgelesen.

_____

b Die Eltern geben **den / die** Mädchen **keinem / kein** Taschengeld.

_____

c Die Schülerin hat **eine / einer** Freundin **eine / einer** Zigarette angeboten.

_____

d Jürgen hat **der / die** Firma **dem / den** Lebenslauf geschickt.

_____

Grammatik

Dative plural nouns

Nouns in the dative plural add an -*n* to the noun except if the nominative plural form already ends in -*n* or -*s*.

sing.	nom. pl.	dat. pl
Mann →	Männer →	Männern
Frau →	Frauen →	Frauen
Foto →	Fotos →	Fotos

Tipp

Now that you have seen all the cases, it is a good idea to memorise the complete tables showing the different endings. Practise them regularly, then you won't have to keep looking them up.

Grammatik

The genitive

This case is the least used of the four cases. Its basic use is to show possession, e.g. 'the girl's bag' can be expressed as *die Tasche des Mädchens* (literally, 'the bag of the girl').

More will be said later about how to use the genitive case (see page 29). For the time being, it is worth recognising its forms:

	masc.	fem.	neut.	plural
the	des	der	des	der
a	eines	eine	eines	–
not a	keines	keiner	keines	keiner

Grammatik

The dative

The indirect object in a sentence is the person or thing to whom or for whom the action of the verb is done, and the dative case is used to show it.

nominative   dative
Der Mann | schickt | der Frau |
accusative
einen Blumenstrauß. The man sends **the woman** a bunch of flowers.

In this sentence, 'the man' is the subject as he is doing the sending, 'a bunch of flowers' is the direct object because it is what is being sent and 'the woman' is the indirect object as she is having the flowers sent <u>to</u> her.

Compare this with:

nominative   accusative
Der Manager | schickt | die Frau | ins Ausland. The manager sends **the woman** abroad.

Here 'the woman' is the direct object (accusative) because she is being sent.

To show the dative case, you need to change the words for 'the', 'a' and 'not a' as follows:

	masc.	fem.	neut.	plural
the	dem	der	dem	den
a	einem	einer	einem	–
not a	keinem	keiner	keinem	keinen

Grammatik

More on the dative

Certain verbs 'trigger' the use of the dative after them:

antworten	to answer	*helfen*	to help
danken	to thank	*schaden*	to harm
folgen	to follow	*schmecken*	to like, to taste of
gefallen	to please	*versprechen*	to promise
gehören	to belong	*vertrauen*	to trust
glauben	to believe	*weh tun*	to hurt
gratulieren	to congratulate		

*Der Schüler hat **der Lehrerin** nicht geantwortet.* The school boy didn't answer the teacher.

*FCKWs schaden **der Umwelt**.* CFCs harm the environment.

---

1 Link the sentence halves so that they make sense and choose the correct option for the dative case.

a Nach dem Fußballspiel hat der Manager

b Die Fischgerichte auf der Speisekarte haben

c Das Handy hat

d Die Lehrerin versucht,

e Da ich den Mann nicht gekannt habe,

f Leider konnte der Arzt

1 **dem** / **die** / **den** Kindern nicht geschmeckt.

2 **dem** / **der** / **die** Jungen nicht gehört.

3 **der** / **die** / **den** Mannschaft gratuliert.

4 **den** / **der** / **die** Leuten nicht helfen.

5 es **den** / **dem** / **die** Schülerinnen zu erklären.

6 habe ich **ihn** / **er** / **ihm** nicht vertraut.

Grammatik

Word order with two objects

Take care over word order in a sentence that has both direct (accusative) and indirect (dative) objects.

When both the direct and indirect objects are nouns, the indirect object goes before the direct object:

indirect object   direct object
Ich gebe einem Freund das Geld.

(An exception to this is if the indirect object person mentioned needs to be emphasised particularly, as in:

*Sie hat ihre Tochter **dem Chef** vorgestellt.* She introduced her daughter to **the boss** [emphasis on the boss].)

If both objects are pronouns (see page 5 for a reminder of pronouns), the direct object goes first:

direct object   indirect object
Ich gebe   es   ihm.

If only one of the objects is a pronoun, it goes before the noun:

pronoun   noun
Ich gebe   ihm   das Geld.
Ich gebe   es   einem Freund.

The rule for the correct word order when using direct and indirect objects can be summarised as follows:

• **Two nouns: dative** comes first.
• **Two pronouns: accusative** comes first.
• **One of each: pronoun** comes first.

---

2 Write the words in the correct order to form complete sentences.

a das Geld / Mein Bruder / gegeben / dem Verkäufer / hat

_____

b Ein Lehrer / es / erklärt / dem Schüler / hat

_____

c bringt / der Frau / Der Mann / einen Blumenstrauß

_____

d hat / den iPod / geliehen / Meine Schwester / mir

_____

e Ich / den tollen Roman / habe / empfohlen / einem Freund

_____

1 **Rewrite the sentences starting with the underlined word or phrase.**

a Meine Mutter fährt <u>jeden Tag</u> zur Arbeit.

_____

b Es gibt keine Bibliothek <u>in unserer Stadt.</u>

_____

c Ich gehe <u>zwei- oder dreimal pro Woche</u> joggen.

_____

d Wir mussten <u>gestern</u> unsere Katze zum Tierarzt bringen.

_____

e Ich war <u>nach zwei Wochen auf Zypern</u> völlig entspannt.

_____

f Meine Familie und ich gehen <u>ab und zu</u> ins Restaurant.

_____

2 **Translate the following sentences into German. Use the words and phrases in the box below to help you.**

a I am going to Majorca next year without my family.

Ich fahre _____ .

b We go into town on foot sometimes.

Wir gehen _____ .

c He went abroad on his own for the first time.

Er ist _____ gefahren.

d I was on a campsite with friends for a week.

Ich war _____ .

in die Stadt   manchmal   auf einem Campingplatz   zu Fuß
zum ersten Mal   nach Mallorca   nächstes Jahr   allein   mit Freunden
eine Woche lang   ins Ausland   ohne meine Familie

3 **Rewrite your sentences from Exercise 2 using inversion. It is up to you what you start the sentences with.**

_____

_____

_____

_____

Grammatik

In simple main clauses

Word order in German has a clear structure and follows a set of rules which you can learn. In a simple sentence, the verb is always the second idea, but this does not mean necessarily that it is the second word, e.g.

1   2
Wir | besuchen | unsere Großeltern.

1   2
Meine Freunde und ich | gehen | später ins Schwimmbad.

Inversion

Almost any part of the sentence can come at the beginning (unlike in English), but the verb is still the second idea and it must then be followed by the subject. Turning the subject and verb around is called **inversion.**

1   2
Am Dienstag | fliegt | der
3
Geschäftsmann | nach Frankfurt.

1   2   3
Außerhalb der Stadt | gibt | es | ein tolles Einkaufszentrum.

Grammatik

Time–Manner–Place

When adverbial expressions of time (e.g. _am Mittwoch_), manner (e.g. _mit dem Auto_) and place (e.g. _nach Stuttgart_) occur <u>after</u> the verb, they must follow this sequence: **Time–Manner–Place.** All three elements don't have to be there, but you still have to keep this order.

          Time
Wir fahren | im Sommer | mit dem
Manner   Place
Reisebus | nach Spanien.

We are travelling to Spain by bus in the summer.

              Time
Mein Onkel arbeitet | nächstes Jahr |
    Place
in Südafrika.

My uncle is working in South Africa next year.

                Manner
Ich gehe | mit meinem besten Freund
  Place
| zur Schule.

I am going to school with my best friend.

1 **Complete the sentences with a co-ordinating conjunction which makes sense.**

a Morgen Nachmittag können wir zu Hause bleiben _____ wir können ins Kino gehen.

b Ich möchte lieber nach Spanien fahren, _____ das Wetter ist dort so schön.

c Morgens stehe ich früh auf _____ ich führe meinen Hund spazieren.

d Sabine geht zum Zahnarzt, _____ sie hat Zahnschmerzen.

e Er ist nicht einkaufen gegangen, _____ er hat im Garten gearbeitet.

2 **Link the sentences with the subordinating conjunctions given in brackets.**

Example: Mein Vater war ganz schön sauer. Ich bin gestern spät nach Hause gekommen. **(weil)**

→ *Mein Vater war ganz schön sauer, weil ich gestern spät nach Hause gekommen bin.*

a Im Moment darf ich nicht fliegen. Ich habe Probleme mit meinen Ohren. **(weil)**

_____

b In der Zukunft wird sie in Deutschland arbeiten. Sie möchte ihre Sprachkenntnisse verbessern. **(da)**

_____

c Mein Bruder fährt sehr gern Rad. Er hat Zeit. **(wenn)**

_____

d Sie wird einen Job suchen. Sie hat die Schule verlassen. **(nachdem)**

_____

e Ich muss meiner Mutter beim Abwaschen helfen. Ich darf ausgehen. **(bevor)**

_____

f Mein Bruder hat viele Freunde kennen gelernt. Er hat in Frankreich gewohnt. **(während)**

_____

g Sie weiß noch nicht. Sie darf morgen auf die Party gehen. **(ob)**

_____

h Wir fahren immer mit der U-Bahn. Wir wollen ins Stadtzentrum fahren. **(wenn)**

_____

3 **Rewrite your answers from Exercise 2 on a separate sheet of paper so that they start with the subordinate clause.**

Example: Mein Vater war ganz schön sauer, weil ich gestern spät nach Hause gekommen bin.

→ *Weil ich gestern spät nach Hause gekommen bin, war mein Vater ganz schön sauer.*

Grammatik

Conjunctions are words which link phrases or sentences together.

Co-ordinating conjunctions

These are *und, aber, denn* (because), *oder* and *sondern* (but – contradicting a negative statement). They are easy to use because they don't affect the word order in the sentence.

Ich bleibe heute zu Hause. + Ich lese einen Roman. → Ich bleibe heute zu Hause und (ich) lese einen Roman.

Er isst kein Fleisch. + Er isst gern Fisch. → Er isst kein Fleisch, aber er isst gern Fisch.

Grammatik

Subordinating conjunctions

Some common subordinating conjunctions are: *weil* (because), *wenn* (when, whenever, if), *da* (since, because), *dass* (that), *bevor* (before), *nachdem* (after), *während* (while), *ob* (whether).

After a subordinating conjunction, the **finite verb** goes to the end of the clause or the end of the sentence:

*Bevor sie zur Schule **geht**, sieht sie gern fern.*

*Wir haben viele Sehenswürdigkeiten besichtigt, während wir in Wien **waren**.*

Notice that it is the **finite verb** (i.e. the part of the verb which changes) that goes to the end.

*Er muss heute Abend zu Hause bleiben, weil er seine Hausaufgaben nicht gemacht **hat**.*

*Mein Freund ist nicht sicher, ob er mich morgen besuchen **wird**.*

*Ich durfte nicht ausgehen, da ich mein Zimmer aufräumen **musste**.*

Tipp

If the subordinate clause starts the sentence, this counts as the first idea in the sentence, so you must remember to invert the verb and subject in the main clause.

       1   2   3
*Da es heute kalt ist, | **trage** | ich Handschuhe.*

1 Complete the sentences with the correct present tense form of the verb given in brackets.

a Heiko _____ diese Seifenoper todlangweilig. (**finden**)

b Zurzeit _____ es fast jeden Tag. Furchtbar! (**regnen**)

c Warum _____ du nicht in einer Werkstätte, wenn du dich für Autos interessierst? (**arbeiten**)

d Das Schild _____ , dass man hier ruhig sein muss. (**bedeuten**)

2 Complete the sentences with the correct present tense form of the verb given in brackets.

a Ich _____ meine Oma am Flughafen _____. (**abholen**)

b Weil die Sendung doof ist, _____ er den Fernseher _____. (**ausschalten**)

c Nächstes Jahr _____ mein Cousin am Schüleraustausch _____ . (**teilnehmen**)

d Jeden Morgen _____ die Kinder so früh _____. (**aufwachen**)

e Der Reisebus _____ immer pünktlich _____. (**abfahren**)

f Abends _____ der Junge stundenlang _____. (**fernsehen**)

3 Decide whether the following verbs are separable or inseparable and write them in the correct column of the table.

separable	inseparable

einladen	gefallen
stattfinden	abfliegen
auskommen	beitragen
widersprechen	umsteigen
besitzen	anbieten
misslingen	zerreißen
weggehen	zuhören
einführen	aufmachen
verlangen	entkommen
empfinden	erwähnen

4 Translate the following sentences into German, using the words in the box at the bottom. Be careful to check whether the verb is separable or not and think about the cases too. Remember that some verbs trigger the use of the dative (see pages 5 and 11.)

a I set off each morning at 8 o'clock. _____

b She is visiting her husband in hospital. _____

c My friends are arriving soon. _____

d I promise him the money. _____

besuchen	abfahren	versprechen	bald	im Krankenhaus	jeden Morgen	ankommen

Grammatik

Present tense endings

How to form the present tense of verbs was looked at on page 6. If the stem ends in *d* or *t*, or in *n* or *m* after a consonant, the letter e must be added before the present tense verb ending -*st* and -*t*.

finden → find- → du findest

antworten → antwort- → er antwortet

zeichnen → zeichn- → du zeichnest

atmen → atm- → ihr atmet

Grammatik

Separable verbs

These have two parts: the verb itself and a separable prefix which splits from the verb and goes to the end of the clause or sentence:

ankommen – to arrive

Der Zug kommt um 8.30 Uhr an – The train arrives at 8.30.

Separable verbs can be weak verbs:

abholen (to fetch, pick up), *anschauen* (to look at), *aufwachen* (to wake up), *ausschalten* (to switch off), *zuhören* (to listen)

or strong verbs:

abfahren (to set off), *anziehen* (to put on), *ausgeben* (to spend), *fernsehen* (to watch TV), *teilnehmen* (to take part)

Grammatik

Inseparable verbs

These are verbs which have a prefix that always stays connected to the verb. They can be either weak or strong. Inseparable prefixes can be seen in:

besuchen (to visit), **emp**fangen (to receive), sich **ent**spannen (to relax), **ge**hören (to belong), **er**fahren (to experience), **miss**verstehen (to misunderstand), **ver**sprechen (to promise), **wider**stehen (to resist), **zer**brechen (to break/smash)

Tipp

To find out whether a separable or inseparable verb is weak or strong, you look up the main part of the verb in a table of strong verbs, e.g. *ankommen, zerbrechen*. Remember that you won't find weak verbs in the table, just strong ones!

Grammatik

It is always a good idea to learn the gender of each noun at the same time as the noun itself. (If you can learn the plural form at the same time, all the better!) There are rules which can help if you can't remember the gender, but there are some exceptions too, so take care.

Masculine *der*
• male people, days of the week, months, seasons, makes of car
• nouns ending in *-el, -er, -ant, -ismus, -ling, -ich, -ist*
Exceptions include: *die Mutter, die Schwester, die Nummer, das Fenster*

Feminine *die*
• female people
• nouns ending in *-ei, -ie, -ung, -ur, -heit, -keit, -tion, -schaft, in, -tät, -enz, -anz*
• many words ending in *-e*
Exceptions include: *der Name, der Käse, der Gedanke, das Auge, das Wochenende*

Neuter *das*
• infinitives used as nouns
• nouns ending in *-chen, -lein, -nis, -o, -um*
Exceptions include: *die Erkenntnis, die Erlaubnis*

1 Indicate whether the following words are masculine, feminine or neuter by writing *der*, *die* or *das* in front. Write the English meaning if you know it. If you aren't sure about the gender or meaning, look it up in a dictionary later to check your answers.

German noun	English
a _____ Datum	
b _____ Hoffnung	
c _____ Hindernis	
d _____ Löffel	
e _____ Enkelin	
f _____ Tourismus	
g _____ Organisation	
h _____ Passant	
i _____ Dunkelheit	
j _____ Erlaubnis	
k _____ Frühling	
l _____ Häuschen	
m _____ Rassismus	
n _____ Tastatur	
o _____ Allianz	

Tipp

If you are writing in German during an exam and need to work out the gender of a noun, it can help to see if you can find it being used in a text elsewhere on the exam paper – but you must check what case it's being used in.

2 What is the gender of these compound nouns? Underline the part of each word which determines the gender, and add *der*, *die* or *das* before it. Then give the meaning in English.

German noun	English
a _____ Geldbeutel	
b _____ Satellitenfernsehen	
c _____ Kontaktbörse	
d _____ Straßenmusikant	
e _____ Verbraucherzufriedenheit	
f _____ Kofferradio	
g _____ Autobahnraststätte	
h _____ Betriebspraktikum	
i _____ Fernsehsender	
j _____ Werbeaktion	

Tipp

Compound nouns are two or more nouns joined together to make one word. This new word always takes its gender from the last part. For example:
der Zahn + die Bürste → die Zahnbürste

■ Topic 1: Qualifiers; The perfect tense

1 Complete each sentence with a different qualifier (which makes sense). Then translate each sentence into English.

a Der Dokumentarkanal hat mir ＿＿＿＿＿ gefallen.

＿＿＿＿＿＿＿＿＿＿＿＿＿＿＿＿＿＿＿＿＿

b Es war ＿＿＿＿＿ unmöglich, den Film zu verstehen.

＿＿＿＿＿＿＿＿＿＿＿＿＿＿＿＿＿＿＿＿＿

c Vor kurzem habe ich ein ＿＿＿＿＿ interessantes Buch gelesen.

＿＿＿＿＿＿＿＿＿＿＿＿＿＿＿＿＿＿＿＿＿

d In unserer kleinen Stadt gibt es ＿＿＿＿＿ Geschäfte.

＿＿＿＿＿＿＿＿＿＿＿＿＿＿＿＿＿＿＿＿＿

e Weil die Straße so nass war, ist sie ＿＿＿＿＿ vorsichtig gefahren.

＿＿＿＿＿＿＿＿＿＿＿＿＿＿＿＿＿＿＿＿＿

f Das Hotel war luxuriös, aber ＿＿＿＿＿ teuer.

＿＿＿＿＿＿＿＿＿＿＿＿＿＿＿＿＿＿＿＿＿

2 Make up three of your own sentences with a different qualifier each time, used in a different way (with a verb, noun, adjective or adverb). Then translate them into English.

＿＿＿＿＿＿＿＿＿＿＿＿＿＿＿＿＿＿＿＿＿

＿＿＿＿＿＿＿＿＿＿＿＿＿＿＿＿＿＿＿＿＿

＿＿＿＿＿＿＿＿＿＿＿＿＿＿＿＿＿＿＿＿＿

＿＿＿＿＿＿＿＿＿＿＿＿＿＿＿＿＿＿＿＿＿

＿＿＿＿＿＿＿＿＿＿＿＿＿＿＿＿＿＿＿＿＿

＿＿＿＿＿＿＿＿＿＿＿＿＿＿＿＿＿＿＿＿＿

3 Complete the sentences with the correct past participle.

a Er hat sich vor dem Frühstück ＿＿＿＿＿ . **(rasieren)**

b Nach den Nachrichten habe ich den Fernseher ＿＿＿＿＿ . **(ausschalten)**

c Das Flugzeug ist rechtzeitig ＿＿＿＿＿ . **(landen)**

d Leider haben sie ihren Wohnwagen＿＿＿＿＿ . **(verkaufen)**

e Weil es so warm war, habe ich das Fenster ＿＿＿＿＿ . **(öffnen)**

f Als er jünger war, ist er nicht besonders gut mit seinem Bruder

＿＿＿＿＿ . **(auskommen)**

g Während wir in den USA waren, haben wir so viele Abenteuer

＿＿＿＿＿ . **(erleben)**

h Nach dem Essen hat meine Schwester alles ＿＿＿＿＿ . **(abtrocknen)**

Grammatik

Qualifiers are used to express how much or how far something is true. They can occur before adjectives, adverbs, verbs or nouns. Learn these commonly used qualifiers and use them to make your sentences more interesting.

sehr	very
ganz	quite
wenig	not very
kaum	hardly, scarcely
wirklich	really
fast	almost
besonders	particularly, especially
recht	quite, very

Dieser Werbespot ist wirklich blöd. This advert is really stupid.

Ich konnte das kaum glauben. I could hardly believe it.

Grammatik

The perfect tense

We have already looked at how to form the perfect tense (see page 7), but there are a few more things you need to know about forming past participles.

If the stem ends in *d* or *t*, or in *n* or *m* after a consonant, the letter *e* must be added before the final -*t* in the past participle:

enden, warten, ordnen, widmen → geendet, gewartet, geordnet, gewidmet

Verbs whose infinitives end in -*ieren* do not add ge- in the past participle:

studieren → studiert

Separable verbs

Both weak and strong separable verbs (see page 14) put ge- between the prefix and the past participle:

aufwachen → aufgewacht

ausgeben → ausgegeben

Inseparable verbs

However, inseparable verbs (see page 14) do not add ge- to the front of the past participle:

versuchen → versucht

beschließen → beschlossen

1 Complete the crossword with the missing past participles from the sentences.

Across

1 Wir haben den Lehrer nicht _____ . (*known*)

2 Meine Familie und ich sind eine Woche in Italien _____ . (*stayed*)

3 Nach dem Überfall sind die Bankräuber einfach _____ . (*disappeared*)

4 Leider hat man sie nie _____ . (*found*)

Down

1 Bis nächste Woche habe ich meiner Freundin 20 € _____ . (*lent*)

2 Der Sportschau-Moderator hat einen hellblauen Anzug _____ . (*wore*)

5 Ich habe an meinen Bruder _____ . (*thought*)

6 Sie haben ihren Sohn Peter _____ . (*named*)

2 Insert the correct past participle in these sentences.

a Hast du ihm das Geld _____? (**geben**)

b Das Mädchen hat ihre neuen Tanzschuhe _____. (**verlieren**)

c Die Sonne hat den ganzen Tag _____. (**scheinen**)

d Ich habe nur vier Stunden _____. (**schlafen**)

e Er hat meinen Bruder nicht _____. (**sehen**)

f Mein Vater hat gar keinen Sport _____. (**treiben**)

g Der Benzinpreis ist schon wieder _____. (**steigen**)

h Sie hat ein Lied auf eine CD _____. (**brennen**)

3 Translate these sentences into German. Take care as there are weak, strong and mixed verbs, together with separable and inseparable verbs. Think about whether to use *haben* or *sein*, and which cases are needed. Some vocabulary is given to help you.

a I rang my uncle last week. _____

b My friend has discovered a mistake. _____

c She has sent no emails today. _____

d We read (*perfect tense*) the article in the newspaper.

_____

e My aunt brought me a present. _____

f He set off at the weekend. _____

g Has the film already started? _____

h We didn't understand the teacher (f). _____

Grammatik

It is important to learn strong verbs from a table, but there are patterns which make the task easier. Study the following patterns; check you know the English meanings too (several of them crop up in the exercises below).

Grammatik

• *nehmen* → *genommen*
schließen → *geschlossen*

Likewise: *bieten, brechen, frieren, genießen, helfen, sprechen, treffen, verlieren, werben, ziehen (gezogen)*

• *finden* → *gefunden*

Likewise: *binden, gelingen, singen, trinken, verschwinden, zwingen*

• *lesen* → *gelesen*

Likewise: *essen (ge**g**essen), fangen, geben, halten, rufen, schlafen, sehen, tragen*

• *schreiben* → *geschrieben*

Likewise: *bleiben, leihen, meiden, scheinen, steigen, treiben*

Grammatik

Mixed verbs are a mixture of weak and strong verbs in that the past participle ends in -*t*, but there is also a vowel change:

brennen → *gebrannt*

bringen → *gebracht*

denken → *gedacht*

kennen → *gekannt*

nennen → *genannt*

rennen → *gerannt*

senden → *gesandt*

wissen → *gewusst*

der Artikel	am Wochenende
verstehen	abfahren
das Geschenk	anfangen
schon	letzte Woche
heute	der Fehler
entdecken	

Grammatik

Indefinite pronouns are the words *jemand* (somebody, someone) and *niemand* (nobody, no-one). They have <u>optional</u> endings to show the cases and are used as follows:

nom.	jemand	niemand
acc.	jemand(*en*)	niemand(*en*)
gen.*	jemand(*e*)s	niemand(*e*)s
dative	jemand(*em*)	niemand(*em*)

Jemand hat meinen Fotopparat gestohlen. (nom.)

Ich habe niemand(en) angerufen. (acc.)

Sie hat jemand(em) ihr Fahrrad geliehen. (dat.)

* The genitive form is seldom used.

1 Complete the sentences with the correct word, showing the ending where appropriate. Remember some verbs are used with the dative case.

a   Hast du _____ gesehen? (*someone*)

b   _____ hat der alten Dame geholfen. (*nobody*)

c   Wir haben _____ am Strand gesehen. (*nobody*)

d   Hallo, ist da _____ ? (*someone*)

e   Er hat _____ den Schlüssel gegeben. (*someone*)

f   _____ interessiert sich für diesen Film. (*nobody*)

g   Mein Vater vertraut _____. (*nobody*)

h   Hat _____ meinen Kuli genommen? (*somebody*)

i   Der alte Mann hat fast den ganzen Tag mit _____ gesprochen. (*nobody*)

j   _____ hat mich gerade angerufen. (*somebody*)

Grammatik

Interrogative adjectives are the word *welch...?* (which ...?) with its different endings. These endings depend on the gender, case and number of the following noun. The endings are as follows:

	masc.	fem.	neuter	plural
nom.	*welcher*	*welche*	*welches*	*welche*
acc.	*welchen*	*welche*	*welches*	*welche*
gen.*	*welches*	*welcher*	*welches*	*welcher*
dat.	*welchem*	*welcher*	*welchem*	*welchen*

Examples:

Welcher Computer ist besser? (nominative)

Welchen Kuli möchten Sie kaufen? (accusative)

In welcher Stadt wohnt er? (*in* + dative here)

* Note that the genitive is rarely used.

> **Tipp**
>
> Notice that the endings used on *welch-* are very similar to those used with the definite article. This should make them easier to remember!

1 Choose the correct option for *welch-* in each sentence.

    a In *welche / welcher / welchem* Haus wohnst du?

    b *Welche / Welcher / Welchen* Fernsehsendungen hat sie gestern gesehen?

    c *Welcher / Welche / Welches* Mannschaft ist die beste?

    d Mit *welchen / welchem / welche*r Bus kommt man am besten dahin?

    e *Welche / Welches / Welche* Buch hast du gerade gelesen?

    f *Welchen / Welcher / Welche* Sänger ist der beste?

    g Aus *welches / welchen / welchem* Land kommen Sie?

    h *Welcher / Welche / Welches* Berg ist höher – der K2 oder der Kilimandscharo?

> **Grammatik**
>
> The endings used on **welch-** are also used for **dies-** (this), **jen-** (that), and **jed-** (each, every).

2 Add the correct endings. Be careful to use the ending with the correct case, number and gender.

    a Herr Müller wollte nicht **jen**_____ Bild kaufen, sondern dieses.

    b **Dies**_____ Fotoapparat funktioniert nicht richtig.

    c Während wir in Rom waren, war **jed**_____ Tag ganz anders.

    d Ich habe **dies**_____ Mann einen Brief geschrieben.

    e In meiner Schule hat **jed**_____ Stunde 45 Minuten gedauert.

    f Nach **dies**_____ langen Woche war sie völlig erschöpft.

    g **Jed**_____ Haus auf der Insel war bunt gestrichen.

    h **Dies**_____ Zug fährt nach Stuttgart und **jen**_____ da hinten nach Bremen.

Grammatik

Active or passive?

Most sentences you have seen so far will have been **active** sentences where the subject (person or thing) <u>does</u> the action of the verb, e.g. My sister found the dog – i.e. my sister (subject) 'did the finding'.

A **passive** sentence is one where the action <u>is done to</u> the subject of the verb, e.g. The dog <u>was found</u> by my sister – i.e. the dog (subject) had 'the finding' done to it.

Note that the passive can be used in all tenses (is found, had been found, will be found, etc.) and that a sentence can be passive without actually naming the person or thing doing the action, as in: A new shopping centre <u>will be opened</u> here next month.

1 After each sentence, write **A** in the box if it is active, and **P** if it is passive.

   a Millions of people use the internet every day. ☐

   b His car was stolen in the town centre. ☐

   c My mother was taken to hospital yesterday. ☐

   d E-mails are delivered almost instantly. ☐

   e My grandparents have just bought a computer. ☐

   f The thieves have been caught by the police. ☐

2 Write in the correct part of *werden* and a past participle as indicated by the phrase in brackets. Use the verbs in the first box below.

   a Sein Handy_____ im Park _____ . (*was found*)

   b Die neuen Lautsprecher _____ heute _____ .
      (*are being delivered*)

   c Unser Sportzentrum _____ vom Bürgermeister
      _____. (*was opened*)

   d Wir _____ durch den Verkehr _____ . (*were held up*)

   e Die Zeitschrift _____ von meiner Mutter _____ .
      (*is being read*)

   f Das Internet _____ zunächst als militärisches Netz
      _____ . (*was developed*)

   g Weil es viel schneit, _____ die Kinder früh nach Hause
      _____ . (*are being sent*)

   h Eine neue Schule _____ dieses Jahr _____ . (*is being built*)

3 Translate these sentences into German, using the vocabulary given in the bottom box on the right.

   a Our school was founded in the 19th century.

   _____

   b The TV was stolen yesterday. _____

   c The car is being bought by my sister. _____

   d Two women were injured in the accident.

   _____

Grammatik

The present passive

In English, the **present passive** is formed using the present tense of the verb 'to be' and a past participle. In German, the present tense of *werden* is used, not *sein*:

ich werde
du wirst
er/sie/es wird
wir werden
ihr werdet
Sie/sie werden
Examples:

*Meine Mutter **wird** ins Ausland **geschickt**.* My mother is (being) sent abroad.

*Die Kuchen **werden verkauft**.* The cakes are (being) sold.

The imperfect passive

To form the **imperfect passive**, simply use the imperfect form of *werden* and a past participle:

ich wurde
du wurdest
er/sie/es wurde
wir wurden
ihr wurdet
Sie/sie wurden

*Die Kuchen **wurden** gestern **verkauft**.* The cakes were sold yesterday.

The word 'by' is translated in three ways:

• *von* + dative (agent)
Das Geschenk wurde <u>von</u> meinem Onkel geschickt.

• *durch* (means)
Der Unfall wurde <u>durch</u> einen Lkw verursacht.

• *mit* + dative (instrument)
Er wurde <u>mit</u> einer Pistole erschossen.

---

aufhalten	schicken
eröffnen	bauen lesen
entwickeln	liefern finden

---

von meiner Schwester

verletzen   im 19. Jahrhundert

bei dem Unfall

die Frau(en) gründen stehlen

der Fernseher

1 Translate these sentences into English.

a Ein Mann ist von einem Auto überfahren worden.

_____

b Ein Adler war gestern im Park gesichtet worden.

_____

c Die E-Mails sind gelöscht worden.

_____

d Neue Maßnahmen waren eingeleitet worden.

_____

e Unser Auto ist heute repariert worden.

_____

f Diese Briefe sind von meiner Schwester geschrieben worden.

_____

g Am Anfang des 20. Jahrhunderts war das Internet noch nicht erfunden worden.

_____

h Ist der Dieb noch nicht erwischt worden?

_____

2 Write the words in the correct order to form complete sentences. Then translate into English.

a muss / bezahlt / einen Monat im Voraus / werden / Die Miete

_____

_____

b werden / nicht / Diese Tatsache / vergessen / darf

_____

_____

c weggeworfen / werden / mussten / Die Äpfel / leider

_____

_____

d muss / werden / Dieses Formular / ausgefüllt / zuerst

_____

_____

e gegen Masern / Alle Kinder / geimpft / sollten / werden

_____

_____

Grammatik

The perfect passive

The perfect passive is made up of the present tense of _sein_ + past participle + _worden_. _Worden_ is the equivalent of 'been' and doesn't change.

Jeder ist von der Werbung beeinflusst worden. Everyone was/has been influenced by the advertising.

The pluperfect passive

The **pluperfect passive** is formed from the imperfect tense of _sein_ + past participle + _worden_.

Jeder war von der Werbung beeinflusst worden. Everyone had been influenced by the advertising.

Grammatik

The passive infinitive

The passive infinitive (the equivalent of 'to be paid/built/done') is formed by using the past participle of the verb, with the infinitive _werden_ (which doesn't change). You will come across it after modal verbs, as in these examples:

Neue Methoden müssen entwickelt werden. New methods must be developed.

Das Auto sollte in München gebaut werden. The car was supposed to be built in Munich.

Grammatik

Prepositions are words which tell you where something is ('in', 'under', etc.). In German, nouns and pronouns following them must always use a certain case, and you need to be confident about whether that should be accusative, dative or genitive each time. (See pages 5, 9–10.)

1 Choose an appropriate accusative preposition to complete the sentences.

   a   Der Zug fährt _____ einen langen Tunnel.

   b   Sonja muss _____ morgen im Krankenhaus bleiben.

   c   Ich bin _____ meinen Pass zum Flughafen gefahren.

   d   Sie hat ein Geschenk _____ ihn gekauft.

2 Choose an appropriate dative preposition to complete the sentences.

   a   Unser Haus steht _____ dem Kino.

   b   Wir wohnen _____ zehn Jahren hier.

   c   Das ist ein Foto _____ ihnen.

   d   _____ der Pause gehen wir ins Labor.

3 Choose the correct word/case in each sentence. If it is possible to use an abbreviation, write it at the end.

   a   Nach dem Film sind wir in **ein / einem** Café gegangen.

   b   Ich habe die Zeitung auf **dem / den** Tisch gelegt.

   c   Der Hund läuft über **die / der** Straße.

   d   In **dem / der** Stadtzentrum waren viele Leute.

   e   Am Samstag bin ich an **dem / das** Meer gefahren.

   f   Die Kinder haben in **das / dem** Meer gespielt.

> ## Tipp
>
> Remember some prepositions can be abbreviated with the definite article:
>
> •   *fürs, ins, ans, aufs*
>
> •   *am, beim, im, vom, zum, zur*

4 Complete the phrase with the correct form of the genitive (see page 29).

   a   wegen d_____ schlechten Wetter____

   b   während d_____ Herbstferien____

   c   innerhalb ein_____ Woche____

   d   trotz ein_____ Unfall____

   e   statt d_____ Kinder____

   f   außerhalb d_____ Geschäftszeiten____

Grammatik

Prepositions followed by the accusative

Mnemonics can be helpful. Think of **FUDGEBOW**:

für (for), *um* (around), *durch* (through), *gegen* (against), *entlang* (along), *bis* (until), *ohne* (without), *wider* (against)

um den Tisch around the table

den Fluß entlang along the river (*entlang* follows the noun)

bis nächstes Jahr until next year

Wider is rare but can appear in phrases like *wider meinen Willen* – against my will.

Grammatik

Prepositions followed by the dative

Think of **MAVS 'N' BAGZ** (or make up your own mnemonic):

mit (with), *ab* (from – time), *von* (of, from), *seit* (since, for), *nach* (after, according to), *bei* (at the house of, with), *aus* (from, out of), *gegenüber* (opposite), *zu* (to)

mit ihm with him

aus dem Haus out of the house

Grammatik

Prepositions followed by the accusative or dative

If no motion is involved, use the dative. If motion is involved, use the accusative.

Er geht in den Garten. (acc.) He goes into the garden. (motion)

Er sitzt in dem/im Garten. (dat.) He is sitting in the garden. (no motion)

Prepositions belonging to this group are:

an, auf, hinter, in, neben, über, unter, vor, zwischen

Grammatik

Prepositions followed by the genitive

Think of **WAITWAS**:

während (during), *außerhalb* (outside of), *innerhalb* (within), *trotz* (in spite of), *wegen* (because of), *anstatt* (instead of), *statt* (instead of)

1 Answer the questions using the future tense and including the time phrase given in brackets. It is up to you where you put the time phrase, but take care with word order.

a Um wie viel Uhr beginnt das Konzert? (**um 19.30 Uhr**)

_____

b Wann fährst du nach Schottland? (**im August**)

_____

c Wie lange bleibt ihr in Italien? (**zehn Tage**)

_____

d Wann kommen deine Eltern nach Hause zurück? (**am Sonntag**)

_____

e Wie lange dauert die Überfahrt? (**etwa anderthalb Stunden**)

_____

f Um wie viel Uhr kommt die Post? (**gegen elf Uhr**)

_____

2 Translate the following sentences into English.

a Der Fernsehapparat wird am Dienstag repariert werden.

_____

b Die Fotos werden bald hochgeladen werden.

_____

c Ein Brief wird von dem Direktor geschickt werden.

_____

d Meine Kinder werden nach dem Film von ihrer Tante abgeholt werden.

_____

e Ein paar Tage vor dem Freilichtkonzert wird die Bühne errichtet werden.

_____

f Hoffentlich wird der Brand bald gelöscht werden.

_____

g Zum Glück werden die alten, leeren Gebäude im Stadtzentrum bald demoliert werden.

_____

h Unsere neue Küche wird morgen eingebaut werden.

_____

Grammatik

To form the **future tense**, use the present tense of _werden_ (see page 20) + an infinitive at the end of the clause or sentence:

Wir werden auf den Markt gehen. We will go/will be going to the market.

Ich werde morgen nicht kommen können. I shall/will not be able to come tomorrow.

Die Zukunft wird weitere technische Fortschritte bringen. The future will bring further technical progress.

The future tense is not used as much in German as it is in English. Instead, the future time frame can be conveyed by a future time indicator (such as 'next week') together with the present tense:

Nächste Woche fliege ich nach Italien. I am flying to Italy next week.

Grammatik

The future passive

In the **passive** (see page 20) the future tense is formed using the relevant part of _werden_ + a past participle + _werden_. (The _werden_ at the end does not change!)

Das neue Kino wird nächsten Monat eröffnet werden. The new cinema will be opened next month.

1 Complete the sentences using the correct passive form.

a Handys _____ in unserer Schule _____ _____ . (*have been banned*)

b Die Probleme mit dem Internet können nicht sofort _____ _____ . (*be solved*)

c Bessere Elektroautos _____ heutzutage _____ . (*are being developed*)

d Immer mehr Zeit _____ vor dem Fernseher _____ . (*is being wasted*)

e Das Handy _____ in den USA _____ . (*was invented*)

f Werbung _____ überall im Internet _____ . (*is watched*)

g Viele Kunden _____ von der Werbung _____ _____ . (*had been manipulated*)

h Leider _____ Handys oft _____ . (*are misused*)

2 Complete the missing case endings.

a Durch d___ Internet gehen viele Arbeitsplätze verloren.

b Es gibt viele Stereotype in d___ Werbung.

c Meine Mutter interessiert sich nicht für d___ Computer.

d Aus dies___ Grund will sie kein___ E-Mails schicken.

e Trotz d___ Gefahren will sie viele Leute online kennen lernen.

f Ich habe ein___ E-Mail von ein___ Freundin in Luxemburg bekommen.

g D___ Junge hat ein___ Handy in d___ Supermarkt gekauft.

h Man klickt auf d___ Maustaste und hat dabei Kontakt zu Menschen überall auf d___ Welt.

i Mit ein___ Computer können wir d___ Lebensmittel einfach online bestellen.

> **Tipp**
>
> These exercises practise some key grammar points you have met in Topic 1 of the Student Book and this Workbook.

3 Write your own sentences, using verbs in the perfect tense.

a Say how long ago you got a mobile phone.

_____

b Say what you last did on the internet.

_____

c Say how much time you spent online last night.

_____

d Say what you liked watching on TV recently.

_____

e Say which recent advertisement you disliked and why.

_____

1 Bringen Sie die Sätze in die richtige Reihenfolge.

1 ___ 2 ___ 3 ___ 4 ___ 5 ___

a Jetzt ist für meine Tochter ein Leben ohne Internet völlig unmöglich.

b Letzten Monat hat sie angefangen, ab und zu im Internet zu chatten.

c Vor zwei Jahren hat sie ihren eignen Laptop bekommen.

d In der Zukunft wird sie versuchen, nicht so lange vor dem PC zu sitzen.

e Schon als kleines Kind konnte meine Tochter einen Computer benutzen.

2 Ergänzen Sie die folgenden zehn Sätze mit der richtigen Verbform.

a Zu viel Zeit vor dem Fernseher _____ die Gesundheit gefährden. (**können**)

b Pro Monat hat das Satellitenfernsehen ziemlich viel _____. (**kosten**)

c Denken ist unnötig, wenn man _____. (**fernsehen**)

d In der Zukunft _____ die Auswahl an Kanälen weiter steigen. (**werden**)

e Die Werbung hat uns über die neuen Produkte _____. (**informieren**)

f Diesen Werbespot werde ich nie _____. (**vergessen**)

g Weil die Werbung etwas geschmacklos war, haben sich einige Leute darüber _____. (**beschweren**)

h Die Zahl der Internet-Benutzer _____ täglich. (**wachsen**)

i Man _____ erst mit 18 Jahren an Internet-Gewinnspielen teilnehmen. (**dürfen**)

j Er hat heute keine SMS-Mitteilungen _____. (**erhalten**)

> ### Tipp
> This is more like the kind of question you will encounter in the exam and is called a cloze test. When filling in a missing verb, check that you know which tense it is – is it a finite verb, or do you need the past participle or infinitive? If it is a finite verb, does it have the correct ending to go with the subject in the sentence?

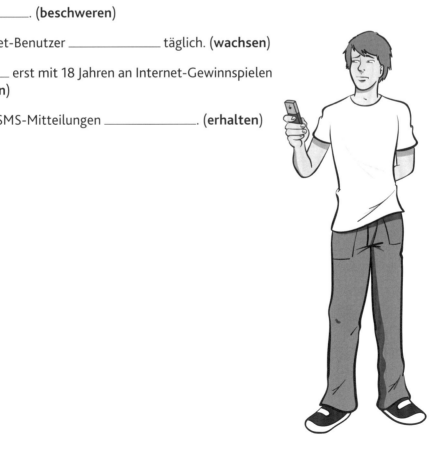

1 To get you thinking about past participles again, circle all the ones you can find in the wordsearch below (weak, strong and mixed). There are 17 in all. Then write them in the correct columns in the table.

Grammatik

Remember (see pages 7, 16–17) that the **perfect tense** is used to refer to an action which happened in the past. It is formed from the present tense of *haben* or *sein* and a past participle. It can have several meanings in English, and it is not necessary to translate the word 'been'.

Mein Lieblingsschauspieler hat in Hollywood gearbeitet. My favourite actor worked/has worked/has been working in Hollywood.

Ich habe ein Buch gelesen. I read/have read /have been reading a book.

n	a	u	s	g	e	z	o	g	e	n	t	z
g	e	g	g	e	s	p	i	e	l	t	a	u
e	r	h	a	l	t	e	n	b	e	s	b	e
r	e	s	p	o	g	e	t	r	a	g	e	n
a	u	s	g	e	s	c	h	a	l	t	e	t
n	b	g	v	i	n	z	a	n	u	g	i	s
n	e	e	e	f	p	g	l	n	g	e	l	c
t	g	e	r	u	f	e	n	t	e	f	t	h
g	o	n	p	s	s	s	m	e	l	r	k	i
e	n	d	a	g	e	e	o	c	e	o	u	e
t	n	e	s	t	u	t	t	a	s	r	l	d
r	e	t	s	j	w	z	z	n	e	e	r	e
a	n	s	t	o	i	t	b	t	n	n	a	n

weak	strong	mixed

2 Choose two verbs from each column and make up a sentence containing each one. Then translate them into English.

_____

_____

_____

_____

_____

_____

Grammatik

The **imperfect tense** is also known as the simple past tense because it consists of only one part. It tends to be used in formal and written German (e.g. a report) whereas the perfect tense is used in spoken and informal situations (e.g. a private letter). However, the imperfect tense of modal verbs (see page 8) and forms of *war* and *hatte*, plus *es gab*, are normally used in conversation too.

The imperfect tense can have several meanings: *ich spielte* – I played, I used to play, I did play, I was playing

Forming the imperfect: weak verbs

Imperfect tense endings are as shown for *kaufen* in the table below. **Weak verbs** use those same endings, but if the stem ends in *d* or *t*, or in *n* or *m* after a consonant, the letter *e* must be added before the actual ending.

ich	kaufte	antwortete	zeichnete	wir	kauften	antworteten	zeichneten
du	kauftest	antwortetest	zeichnetest	ihr	kauftet	antwortetet	zeichnetet
er/sie/es	kaufte	antwortete	zeichnete	Sie/sie	kauften	antworteten	zeichneten

1 Add the correct endings to these weak verbs.

a Sie **erzähl**___ ihrem Sohn eine Geschichte.

b Wir **kauf**___ Wurst und Pommes.

c Um 23 Uhr **land**___ meine Freunde in Spanien.

d Ich **besuch**___ meine Tante am Wochenende.

e Du **antwort**___ nicht.

f Der Film **dauer**___ fast zweieinhalb Stunden und **end**___ kurz vor Mitternacht.

g Steffi **zeig**___ mir ihren neuen Kopfhörer.

h Meine Familie und ich **amüsier**___ uns im Freizeitpark.

i Er **studier**___ Jura und Psychologie in Berlin.

Tipp

When you are reading in German, look closely at the verb endings. It is easy to tell the difference between the present and the imperfect tense – look for the extra *t* or *te* in the imperfect.

2 Translate these sentences into German using verbs in the imperfect tense. Use the vocabulary below to help you.

a The tickets cost nothing.

_____

b We lived abroad.

_____

c I heard a noise.

_____

d The girls were laughing loudly.

_____

e It rained yesterday.

_____

f We were waiting for (*auf* + acc) the train.

_____

laut	das Geräusch	kosten
der Zug	lachen	nichts
warten	die Karten	regnen
hören	im Ausland	

Topic 2: The imperfect tense: strong verbs, mixed verbs

1 Circle the 10 imperfect stems (strong verbs) in the wordsearch. Note them in the list at the side.

e	m	p	f	a	h	l
s	c	t	i	n	a	i
a	s	a	n	g	l	e
h	e	t	g	a	f	f
s	t	a	n	d	h	t
g	e	w	a	n	n	m

_____

_____

_____

_____

_____

_____

_____

_____

_____

_____

Grammatik

Forming the imperfect: strong verbs

For **strong verbs**, you need to learn the imperfect stem (from a strong verb table) and add the endings shown for *kommen*:

kommen → *kam-*
ich	kam
du	kamst
er/sie/es	kam
wir	kamen
ihr	kamt
Sie/sie	kamen

Forming the imperfect: mixed verbs

Mixed verbs are a combination. You need the imperfect stem (with its vowel change), with the endings for weak verbs, e.g. *ich wusste, er rannte, wir kannten, sie dachte, sie brachten, wir nannten, sie sandte, es brannte.*

Tipp

Some verbs are used in the imperfect tense in speech and informal situations. These include the different forms of *hatte* (had) and *war* (was) together with the phrase *es gab* (there was, there were).

Tipp

Don't forget that the *ich* and *er/sie/es* forms of strong verbs don't add any ending to the imperfect stem!

2 Complete the following sentences with the completed imperfect verbs whose stems you found in the wordsearch.

a Wir _____ 20 Minuten an der Bushaltestelle. (*stood*)

b Die Kellnerin _____ die Hühnersuppe. (*recommended*)

c Die Kinder _____ an zu weinen.
(*started* < **anfangen**)

d Der Skifahrer _____ eine Silbermedaille. (*won*)

e Ich _____ unserer Nachbarin im Garten. (*helped*)

f Karla und Birgit _____ im Schulchor. (*sang*)

g Er _____ die Tabletten dreimal am Tag. (*took*)

h Nach der Arbeit _____ ihm die Muskeln weh. (*hurt*)

i Der Hund _____ aus dem Haus. (*ran*)

j Letzte Woche _____ meine Freundin und ich unsere Lieblingsgruppe. (*saw*)

Grammatik

The genitive case is used to show possession. Where we use sentences in English with 's, they have to be turned around in German:

genitive

The man's car is very old → The car <u>of the man</u> is very old.

genitive

My uncle's dog is called Max → The dog <u>of my uncle</u> is called Max.

In German, you show the genitive case by changing the words for 'the', 'a', 'my', etc. as shown in the table:

	masc.	fem.	neut.	plural
the	des	der	des	der
a	eines	einer	eines	–
not a	keines	keiner	keines	keiner
my	meines	meiner	meines	meiner

A word for 'of' is not needed. However, you have to add -s or -es to most masculine and neuter nouns. The choice between -s and -es can depend on how easy it is to pronounce the word, but -es must be added with words ending in -s, -ß, -x, -z: *meines Hauses, des Krebses, des Kreuzes*. This ending also often occurs with words ending in -sch, -st, -zt: *des Tisches, eines Arztes*.

The ending -s is normal with words ending in a vowel: *des Schnees*, and many other words: *des Abends, des Königs, des Lehrers*.

No ending is needed on a feminine noun: *Der Ring ein<u>er</u> Frau wurde gefunden*.
but: *Der Hund mein<u>es</u> Onkels heißt Max*.

1 Complete the sentences with the correct genitive endings. Add -s or -es to the noun when appropriate.

a Die Katze mein____ Freundin____ ist schwarz und weiß.

b Am Ende d____ Konzert____ gingen wir nach Hause.

c Das Porträt ein____ Musiker____ hing in der Galerie.

d Das Zimmer mein____ Schwester____ sieht immer so ordentlich aus.

e Ich habe nur die ersten zwei Seiten d____Roman____ gelesen.

f Wir konnten die Mutter d____ Kinder____ nicht finden.

g Sie hat ein Bild ein____ Auto____ gezeichnet.

h Man konnte die Namen d____ Schauspielerinnen____ nicht lesen.

2 Translate these phrases into German, using the words in the box below to help you.

a because of the internet _____

b instead of a mobile phone _____

c during the advert break _____

d in spite of the problems _____

e because of the weather _____

f during the summer _____

> **Tipp**
> Possessive adjectives (*mein, dein*, etc.) add the same endings as *ein* and *kein*. (See pages 9–10.)

> **Tipp**
> In speech, the genitive is seldom used to indicate possession. Instead, the word 'of' is translated with *von* + dative:
> *Das ist ein Foto <u>von meinem Bruder</u>.*

> **Grammatik**
> Remember that the genitive case is used after certain prepositions (see page 22) such as *während* (during), *(an)statt* (instead of), *wegen* (because of), *trotz* (in spite of), e.g. *während <u>des</u> Konzert<u>s</u>* – during the concert.
> Be aware that these groups are not always clear-cut; for example, you may come across *wegen* and *trotz* followed by the dative.

> **Tipp**
> The genitive is also used to express an indefinite time (*eines Tages, eines Nachts* – feminine!), manner (*ich fahre immer zweiter Klasse*), and in certain expressions (*ich bin der Meinung, es ist der Mühe wert*).

> die Werbepause das Wetter der Sommer das Problem(-e) das Handy das Internet

■ Topic 2: Comparative and superlative adjectives

1 Translate the following comparative and superlative adjectives into German.

a longer _____

b biggest _____

c more beautiful _____

d nearest _____

e latest _____

f nicer _____

g fastest _____

h more sensible _____

i poorest _____

j funnier _____

2 Complete the sentences with the superlative form of the adjective given in brackets. Check the ending is also correct.

a Wir sind mit dem _____ Zug der Welt gefahren. (**schnell**)

b Das war der _____ Tag meines Lebens. (**gut**)

c Ich habe auf der _____ Insel übernachtet. (**schön**)

d Wegen der Wolken konnte man die _____ Gebäude nicht sehen. (**hoch**)

e Die _____ Apotheke befindet sich in der Hauptstraße. (**nah**)

f Sie ist nicht die _____ Person. (**intelligent**)

3 Write sentences in German comparing the following things. Use your own adjectives.

a Bayern München – Chelsea _____

b Salat – Pommes frites _____

c Venedig – Paris _____

d 'Skyfall' – 'Avatar' _____

4 Compare the pairs of things in Exercise 3 using *nicht so … wie*.

_____

_____

_____

_____

5 Write three sentences of your own using the comparative + *als*, and three more sentences using *nicht so … wie*. Compare two actors, two types of music and two books. Use a different adjective each time.

_____

_____

_____

_____

_____

_____

Grammatik

Comparative

In English, we compare things either by adding '-er' to the adjective ('small<u>er</u>') or sometimes we need to use 'more …' ('<u>more</u> interesting'). In German, 'more' is not used in this situation; just add *-er* to a German adjective to form the **comparative adjective**:

Der Film ist interessanter als das Buch. The film is more interesting than the book.

Superlative

The **superlative adjective** ('small<u>est</u>', '<u>most</u> interesting') is formed by adding *-(e)ste* to a German adjective. If the adjective precedes the noun, it needs the correct adjectival ending too (see page 55).

der klein<u>ste</u> Hund the smallest dog

die interessant<u>esten</u> Fernsehsendungen the most interesting television programmes

Grammatik

Most adjectives with one syllable have an umlaut in the comparative and superlative forms:

alt → *älter* → *älteste*
groß → *größer* → *größte*

Some are irregular so need to be learned:

gut → *besser* → *beste*
hoch → *höher* → *höchste*
nah → *näher* → *nächste*
viel → *mehr* → *meiste*

Tipp

If you want to say someone/something is 'not as … as' someone/something else, use the phrase *nicht so* + adjective + *wie*: *Er ist <u>nicht so</u> intelligent <u>wie</u> sie*. He is not as intelligent as her.

Grammatik

Present tense

We looked at using modal verbs in the imperfect tense on page 8. Here we shall check how to use them in two other tenses. They tend to be used with another verb (in the infinitive form at the end of the sentence), but are sometimes used on their own.

The six modal verbs are irregular but follow a similar pattern to each other. Learn the **present tense** forms in the table below.

	dürfen	*können*	*mögen*	*müssen*	*sollen*	*wollen*	
ich	*darf*	*kann*	*mag*	*muss*	*soll*	*will*	*Er darf nicht rauchen.* He is not allowed to/must not smoke.
du	*darfst*	*kannst*	*magst*	*musst*	*sollst*	*willst*	*Sie können Französisch (sprechen).* They can speak French.
er/sie/es	*darf*	*kann*	*mag*	*muss*	*soll*	*will*	*Du musst fleißig arbeiten.* You must/have to work hard.
wir	*dürfen*	*können*	*mögen*	*müssen*	*sollen*	*wollen*	*Sie sollen nächstes Jahr nach China fahren.*
ihr	*dürft*	*könnt*	*mögt*	*müsst*	*sollt*	*wollt*	They shall/are to/are supposed to go to China next year.
Sie/sie	*dürfen*	*können*	*mögen*	*müssen*	*sollen*	*wollen*	*Ich mag dieses Lied.* I like this song.
							Wollt ihr alles sehen? Do you want to see everything?

1 Complete the sentences with the correct present tense form of the modal verb given in brackets.

a Meine Schwester _____ nicht zu spät ausgehen. (**dürfen**)

b Du _____ das nicht machen. (**sollen**)

c Wir _____ klassische Musik. (**mögen**)

d Heute Abend _____ ich mit Freunden ausgehen. (**wollen**)

e Ihr _____ diesen Film unbedingt sehen! (**müssen**)

f Meine Eltern _____ diesen Sänger nicht leiden. (**können**)

g Ich _____ morgen zum Zahnarzt gehen. (**sollen**)

h _____ er vielleicht am Freitag kommen? (**können**)

2a Translate these sentences into English.

a Ich habe einen Brief schreiben müssen. _____

b Er hat nach Hause gehen dürfen. _____

c Wir haben jeden Tag schwimmen können. _____

d Haben deine Freunde nicht mitkommen wollen? _____

2b Without looking at the original German sentences (cover them up!), translate your sentences from Exercise 2a back into German.

_____ _____

_____ _____

3 Rewrite the following sentences using the perfect tense of the modal verb.

a Mein Neffe durfte gestern Abend nicht fernsehen.

_____

b Wir wollten heute ins Theater gehen.

_____

c Ich musste den Arzt anrufen.

_____

d Konntest du das Schild nicht lesen?

_____

Tipp

Notice that the singular forms (*ich*, *du*, and *er/sie/es*) of modal verbs in the present tense never have an umlaut.

Tipp

Be careful never to translate 'I have to' and 'I had to' with *ich habe*, *ich hatte*. Always use *ich muss, ich musste*.

Grammatik

Perfect tense

To form the **perfect tense**, if the modal verb is used alone, you need its past participle: *gedurft, gekonnt, gemocht, gemusst, gesollt, gewollt*.

Ich habe das nicht gewollt. I didn't want that.

However, if the modal verb is used with another verb, you must use the infinitive form instead of the past participle:

Wir haben unsere Großeltern nicht besuchen können. We have not been able to visit our grandparents.

Tipp

The auxiliary verb used with a modal verb in the perfect tense is always *haben* because it refers to the modal verb and not to the other verb.

◼ Topic 2: Possessive adjectives

1 Choose the correct form of the possessive adjective.

a **Meine / Mein / Meinen** Vater hat **sein / seine / seinen** Autoschlüssel verloren.

b Ich habe **meiner / meine / meinen** Schwester **ihre / ihren / ihr** Handy zurückgegeben.

c **Sein / Seine / Seiner** Schwester hat **ihr / ihren / ihres** Zimmer aufgeräumt.

d **Mein / Meinen / Meine** Buch liegt auf dem Tisch neben **meine / meinem / mein** Bett.

e Der Junge hat **sein / seinen / seinem** Examen in Englisch bestanden.

f In **unser / unserer / unseren** Garage steht **mein / meine / meiner** Fahrrad.

g Während **ihre / ihren / ihrer** Schulferien haben die Kinder sehr viel unternommen.

h Gegenüber **seinen / seinem / sein** Haus steht **unserer / unsere / unser** Kirche.

2 Complete the sentences with the correct form of the possessive adjective.

a Wir haben _____ Haus verkauft. (*our*)

b _____ Kuli war in _____ Tasche. (*my, her*)

c Das Geschenk für _____ Vater ist unter _____ Bett versteckt. (*our, my*)

d Martin und Silke, habt ihr _____ Hausaufgaben gemacht? (*your*)

e _____ Mutter hat ein Foto von _____ Oma gemacht. (*my, our*)

f _____ Lehrerin hat _____ Eltern angerufen. (*our, their*)

g Wegen _____ Dummheit hat er _____ Bus verpasst. (*his, his*)

h _____ Katze ist in _____ Garten gelaufen. (*your – polite, our*)

i _____ Freunde konnten _____ neues Haus nicht finden. (*our, your – familiar sing.*)

j Zurzeit wohnt _____ ältester Bruder bei _____ Freundin in Frankfurt. (*my, his*)

1 Unscramble the words to make sentences. Start with the underlined word or phrase.

a verbracht / in Wien / haben / Zu Ostern / eine Woche / wir

_____

b mein Cousin / wird / Bald / fliegen / in die Schweiz

_____

c mit der Straßenbahn / ich / gefahren / zum ersten Mal / bin / Heute

_____

d einen Stau / es / jeden Tag / Auf dieser Autobahn / gibt

_____

e im See / geschwommen / Er / mit seinen Freunden / während der Ferien / ist

_____

f habe / in der Stadtmitte / getroffen / ich / meine Freunde / Danach

_____

2 Link the sentences using the conjunction or question word given in brackets. In items d and g, omit (es) as it is no longer necessary.

Example: _Wir möchten Andenken kaufen. Wir fliegen morgen nach Hause._ **(bevor)**
Wir möchten Andenken kaufen, bevor wir morgen nach Hause fliegen.

a Markus sieht gern Filme. Er geht nicht so oft ins Kino. **(aber)**

_____

b Ich weiß nicht. Der Zug fährt ab. **(wann)**

_____

c Willst du immer noch ausgehen? Es ist heute so kalt. **(obwohl)**

_____

d Er hat (es) nicht gehört. Sie hat (es) gesagt. **(was)**

_____

e Die Kinder sind sofort nach Hause gegangen. Sie wollten mit ihrem Hund spielen. **(denn)**

_____

f Wir haben uns noch nicht entschieden. Wir werden auf dem Campingplatz bleiben. **(wie lange)**

Tipp
Don't forget that separable verbs join up again in a subordinate clause, e.g.
stattfinden – es findet statt – Wir wissen nicht, wo das Konzert am Freitag stattfindet.

Grammatik
The main points regarding word order in a sentence were covered on pages 12–13. To re-cap the basic principles:

In a **main clause**, the verb is the **second idea**, e.g.

| 1 | 2 | |
Mein Vater | geht | heute ins Büro.

You can start with other parts of the sentence which aren't the subject, but you must make sure that the verb is still the second idea and that you use **inversion** for the subject and verb, e.g.

| 1 | 2 | |
Heute | geht | mein Vater ins Büro.

Use the order **Time – Manner – Place** when these expressions are used after the verb, e.g.

Time   Manner
Ich fahre | am Samstag | mit dem
Place
Bus |in die Stadt.

Tipp
Make sure that you use inversion after words such as these which commonly start sentences:

glücklicherweise	fortunately
zum Glück	fortunately
leider	unfortunately
zuerst	first(ly)
schließlich	finally
zum Schluss	finally
bald	soon
später	later
zurzeit	at present
damals	at that time
danach	afterwards
früher	earlier
vorher	before(hand)
inzwischen	meanwhile

Grammatik
Co-ordinating conjunctions (_und, aber, denn, oder, sondern_) do not affect the word order in a sentence:

Das Haus ist sehr alt und (es) befindet sich auf dem Land.

Subordinating conjunctions (_weil, da, dass, wenn, als, bevor, obwohl, sobald,_ etc.) make the finite verb go to the end of the clause or sentence:

Er mag diese Band, da er ihre Musik immer inspirierend gefunden hat.

This word order is also used after a question word (_wann, was, wo, wie, warum_) in an indirect question:
Ich weiß nicht genau, wo in Berlin er wohnt.

1 Turn these statements into questions by changing the word order as necessary.

  a Mein Onkel ruft heute Abend an.

  _____

  b Sie konnte den Brief nicht lesen.

  _____

  c Das Paket für mich ist schon angekommen.

  _____

  d Du hast ihn gestern Vormittag gesehen.

  _____

  e Sein Bruder darf keine Erdnüsse essen.

  _____

  f Ilse und ihre Familie sind noch einen Tag geblieben.

  _____

  g Man muss dieses lange Formular ausfüllen.

  _____

  h Das Konzert fängt um halb acht an.

  _____

2 Write questions which will produce these answers. There may be more than one correct way to do this.

  a _____?

  Ich möchte drei oder vier Jahre in Deutschland arbeiten.

  b _____?

  Nein, ich habe diese Sendung nicht gesehen.

  c _____?

  Weil ihr Auto kaputt ist.

  d _____?

  Der Film wird in Norwegen gedreht.

  e _____?

  Sie ist eine der berühmtesten Schauspielerinnen der Welt.

  _____?

  f Nein, das Musikfestival fand vor zwei Wochen statt.

3 Make up questions using the question words which you didn't use in Exercise 2.

  _____

  _____

  _____

Grammatik

There are two ways of making a question in German.

- Start the sentence with the (finite) verb followed by the subject:
  Du hast einen Hund → *Hast du einen Hund?*
  Der Film hat schon begonnen → *Hat der Film schon begonnen?*
- Start with a specific question word:
  wer who
  wann when
  wo where   *wohin* where (to)
      woher where from
  wie how   *wie viel* how much
      wie viele how many
      wie lange how long
  welcher/welche/welches which
  was what   *was für* what kind of
  warum why   *wieso* why

Examples:
Wer wohnt in diesem Haus? Who lives in this house?
Wann hast du den Pulli gekauft? When did you buy the pullover?

Tipp

When making questions in German, you don't have to think about using a word for 'do', 'does' or 'did' because they aren't used. Just concentrate on getting the word order correct.

Tipp

Be careful to get the correct word for 'where'. Sometimes in English, we mean to say 'where to' but omit the 'to', e.g. 'Where are you going (to)?' In German, you must use *wohin* for this, not just *wo*.

Wohin and *woher* can sometimes be split, without changing the meaning:
Wohin gehst du? = Wo gehst du hin?
Woher kommst du? = Wo kommst du her?

Tipp

Don't mix up *wann* and *wenn*. In a direct or indirect question, always use *wann*. Otherwise use *wenn*.

Wann endet der Film? Ich weiß nicht, wann der Film endet.
Ich lese gern, wenn ich Zeit habe.

1 Translate these sentences into German. Take care with word order.

a He is coming next Friday.

_____

b The wine costs 20 € a bottle.

_____

c We stayed one night.

_____

d The baby is only (*erst*) one month old.

_____

e We bought the car last February.

_____

f Every Wednesday she visits her grandad.

_____

2 Complete the sentences with the correct dative form of the missing word, and translate them into English.

a Hast du _____ den Fuß verrenkt?

_____

b Ich war d_____ Arzt sehr dankbar.

_____

c Birgit ist ihr_____ Mutter ähnlich.

_____

d Diese Frau war _____ nicht bekannt. (*him*)

_____

e Ein Fremder hat _____ das Leben gerettet. (*her*)

_____

3 Translate these sentences into German.

a I am so cold. _____

b We are sorry. _____

c He doesn't care. _____

d They are warm. _____

Grammatik

The cases have been looked at already (see pages 9–11), but it is very important that you keep practising using them in different situations.

The nominative case is used for the subject of the sentence. The accusative is for the direct object, and the dative is for the indirect object.

nominative · · · · · · · · dative
Mein Vater | kauft | meiner Mutter |

accusative
eine Schachtel Pralinen.

Tipp

There are accusative and dative endings for articles, pronouns and adjectives; it's essential to learn the patterns so that you use them automatically. See pages 55 and 56.

Grammatik

Accusative

The accusative is used after certain prepositions (see page 22). It is also used:
- to show a duration of time or express a distance:
  Ich bin einen Monat geblieben.
  Er ging einen Schritt weiter.
- when talking about quantities:
  Es kostet zehn Euro das Kilo/die Flasche/das Stück.
- when referring to a definite time:
  jeden Mittwoch, nächsten Monat.

Grammatik

Dative

The dative is used with certain prepositions and verbs (see pages 11, 22). It is also used to show possession, when referring to parts of the body:

Ich habe mir den Arm gebrochen.
I've broken my arm.

It is used after certain adjectives which follow the noun: *ähnlich* – similar to, *bekannt* – known to, *dankbar* – grateful to, *nützlich* – useful to.

Meine Mutter war meinem Vater sehr dankbar.

It is also used in certain idiomatic phrases, such as:

Mir ist warm/kalt/schlecht. I feel warm/cold/sick.

Es tut ihm Leid. He is sorry.
Es ist ihnen egal. They don't mind.

1 Complete the missing case endings.

a Ich schicke mein_____ Cousine dies_____ Foto von mein _____ Hund.

b Nach d_____ Sommerferien will ich ein_____ Computer kaufen.

c Letzt_____ April ist sie in d_____ Alpen Ski gefahren.

d Ihr _____ Katze schläft neben d_____ Kommode in ihr_____ Schlafzimmer.

e Während unser_____ Aufenthalt_____ in d_____ Schweiz haben wir ein_____ Tag in Genf verbracht.

f Trotz d_____ Regen_____ hat er kein_____ Regenmantel getragen.

g D_____ Mädchen hat d_____ Einkaufsliste in d_____ Tasche gesteckt.

> **Tipp**
> These exercises practise the grammar points you have met in the second section of the book.

2 Fill in the gaps with adjectives in the superlative.

a Die Donau ist der _____ Fluss Österreichs. (**lang**)

b Das war der _____ Tag seines Lebens. (**schlimm**)

c Er ist der _____ Schauspieler Hollywoods. (**erfolgreich**)

d Der _____ Berg Deutschlands ist die Zugspitze. (**hoch**)

e Heiko war der _____ Schüler in seiner Klasse. (**jung**)

f Anna ist meine _____ Freundin. (**gut**)

3 Read the text and fill in the gaps with verbs in the imperfect tense.

Gestern Abend _____ es einen Unfall in unserer Straße.

(**geben**) Eine alte Dame _____ von einem Radfahrer überfahren.

(**werden**) Leider _____ sie nicht gut sehen (**können**) und

_____ den Radfahrer zu spät. (**sehen**) Zum Glück _____

sie keine Verletzungen, (**haben**) sie _____ nur etwas

schockiert. (**sein**) Trotzdem _____ sie ein Krankenwagen ins

Krankenhaus. (**bringen**) Ein Arzt _____ sie (**untersuchen**) und

sie _____ dort übernachten (**müssen**), aber am nächsten Tag

_____ sie wieder nach Hause gehen. (**dürfen**)

1 Ergänzen Sie die folgenden zehn Sätze mit der richtigen Verbform.

a Mozart _____ Musik im 18. Jahrhundert. (**komponieren**)

b Nach dem Konzert hat meine Mutter eine CD von der Vorstellung

  kaufen _____. (**wollen**)

c Meine Eltern finden diesen Musikstil wunderbar, aber er

  _____ meinem Bruder gar nicht. (**gefallen**)

d Im 20. Jahrhundert _____ neue Technologien neue Klänge

  und Töne. (**bringen**)

e Musikfestivals im Freien gefallen mir, weil ich die frische Luft

  _____. (**genießen**)

f Ich fühle mich wohl, wenn ich modische Kleidung _____.

  (**anziehen**)

g Levi Strauss _____ aus Deutschland und _____ in

  San Francisco. (**kommen**, **sterben**)

h Heutzutage _____ Ökomode immer beliebter. (**werden**)

i Vor drei Monaten _____ dieser japanische Designer ein tolles

  Kleid für sie entwerfen. (**sollen**)

j Die Supermodels waren nicht besonders schön, weil sie alle

  magersüchtig _____. (**aussehen**)

> **Tipp**
> Remember to check which tense
> is needed: look at the sentence for
> clues such as time phrases. Think
> also about who or what is the
> subject of the verb, so that you can
> work out the right ending.

2 Lesen Sie diese Bemerkungen über Image und wählen Sie jeweils die Ergänzung, die am besten passt.

Ist Image wichtig?

a Ich meine, dass jeder _____ eigenen Stil haben sollte.
 i sein   ii seine   iii seinen

b Wenn man zu einem Interview geht, _____ man einen guten Eindruck machen.
 i müssen   ii musst   iii muss

c Die Kleidung ist nicht so wichtig _____ die Person selbst.
 i als   ii wie

d Wenn ich alte Klamotten trage, ...
 i dann bin ich richtig entspannt. ii dann ich richtig entspannt bin. iii dann ich bin richtig entspannt.

e Bevor ich zu einem Date gehe, überlege ich immer, _____ ich anziehen soll.
 i wie   ii was   iii warum

f Mein Image war mir egal – Markenkleidung _____ ich uninteressant. Jetzt kaufe ich aber nur noch schicke Kleidung!
 i findet   ii fand   iii fandet

g Ich finde es unattraktiv, dass die Tochter _____ immer so schlampig ist.
 i des Lehrers   ii dem Lehrer   iii der Lehrer

h ... sollte man unbedingt das richtige Image haben.
 i Wenn will man cool aussehen,   ii Wenn man will cool aussehen,   iii Wenn man cool aussehen will,

Topic 3: Modal verbs

1 Identify whether these modal verbs are indicative (I) or subjunctive (S), or could be either (IS).

a mochtest ☐   b müsste ☐   c solltest ☐   d dürften ☐

e konnte ☐   f wollten ☐   g mochtet ☐   h dürftet ☐

i könnten ☐   j sollte ☐

2 Complete the sentences with the correct form of the imperfect subjunctive of the modal verb in brackets. Then translate each sentence into English.

a Gabi _____ ins Kino gehen. **(dürfen)**

_____

b Wir _____ uns vielleicht später treffen. **(können)**

_____

c Meine Freunde _____ mitkommen. **(mögen)**

_____

d Wie hart _____ ich trainieren? **(müssen)**

_____

e Ab morgen _____ ich mich regelmäßig bewegen. **(mögen)**

_____

f Wann _____ ihr vorbeikommen? **(können)**

_____

3 Complete the sentences by choosing the correct type of imperfect modal verb.

a Gestern Nachmittag **musste / müsste** ich zum Arzt gehen.

b Nächste Woche **konnten / könnten** wir die Eintrittskarten für das Konzert abholen.

c Ich **mochte / möchte** dich morgen sehen.

d **Konntest / könntest** du das Waschpulver nicht finden, als du im Supermarkt warst?

e Die Kinder **durften / dürften** diese Süßigkeiten nicht essen, weil sie schlecht für die Zähne waren.

f Ich habe so einen Hunger – ich **konnte / könnte** noch eine Portion Kartoffeln essen!

Grammatik

Imperfect tense and imperfect subjunctive

We looked at modal verbs on pages 8 and 31. Here we are focusing on the **imperfect indicative** (i.e. the 'normal' imperfect) and the **imperfect subjunctive** forms of modal verbs.

Two modal verbs, **wollen** and **sollen**, are exactly the same in the imperfect subjunctive and the imperfect indicative:

	wollen	sollen
ich	wollte	sollte
du	wolltest	solltest
er/sie/es	wollte	sollte
wir	wollten	sollten
ihr	wolltet	solltet
Sie/sie	wollten	sollten

For the other four verbs, you form the imperfect subjunctive by adding an umlaut to the imperfect indicative, as in the following examples:

	imperfect (indicative)	conditional (imperfect subjunctive)
ich	mochte	möchte
du	konntest	könntest
er/sie/es	durfte	dürfte
wir	mussten	müssten
ihr	konntet	könntet
Sie/sie	mochten	möchten

The imperfect subjunctive conveys the idea of 'would':

ich möchte I would like (to)

wir müssten we would have to

The imperfect subjunctive of *sollen*, *müssen* and *dürfen* can also convey the idea of 'ought to' or 'should':

Der Zug müsste da sein. The train should be there.

Das dürfte wohl reichen. That ought to be enough.

Tipp

Take great care when translating the word 'could' into German because it can mean both 'was able' and 'would be able' (different tenses), so think carefully about whether to choose *konnte* (referring to past) or *könnte* (referring to future possibility).

Grammatik

In some constructions in German, the infinitive is used with *zu* at the end of the clause. This is called an **infinitive clause**.

*Es begann **zu regnen**.* It started to rain.
*Ich habe versprochen, den Hund **zu füttern**.* I promised to feed the dog.

If you need to use *zu* with a separable verb, it goes between the separable prefix and the verb itself, <u>as one word</u>.

*Es ist mir gelungen, die Tür richtig **zuzumachen**.* I managed to close the door properly.

1 Read these sentences and insert *zu* if necessary.

a Wir mussten ganz früh _____ aufstehen.

b Obwohl ich mich müde fühle, will ich noch nicht ins Bett _____ gehen.

c Morgen versuche ich, die Waschmaschine _____ reparieren.

d Du musst versprechen, mir eine E-Mail _____ schicken.

e Ich wollte das Fenster auf _____ machen, weil es so warm war.

f Er hat vergessen, sein Zimmer _____ putzen.

g Es hat jetzt aufgehört _____ schneien.

h Mein bester Freund will kein Fleisch _____ essen.

2 Complete these sentences using the appropriate infinitive clause. Use the words in the box below to help you.

a Ich gehe morgen ins Einkaufszentrum, _____.

([in order] to buy a shirt)

b Wir möchten Spaß haben, _____.

(without wasting too much money)

c Sie surft im Internet, _____.

(instead of watching TV)

d Er ist zu jung, _____.

([in order] to understand everything)

e Die Leute haben nichts gemacht, _____.

(instead of ringing the police)

f Wir sind ausgegangen, _____.

(without locking the front door)

Tipp

Remember, if a modal verb is being used, you don't need to add *zu* at all.

Er musste eine Reservierung machen. He had to make a reservation.

Sie wollen den Hund füttern. They want to feed the dog.

Er muss seinen Vater anrufen. He has to phone his father.

Grammatik

There are other instances when *zu* can be used with the infinitive:

um ... zu in order to do
*Ich jogge jeden Tag, **um** fit **zu** werden.*

ohne ... zu without doing
*Er ist eingeschlafen, **ohne** den Fernseher aus**zu**schalten.*

anstatt ... zu instead of doing
*Sie trifft lieber ihre Freundinnen, **anstatt** im Haushalt **zu** helfen.*

Tipp

Remember that if the sentence starts with an infinitive clause, it is followed by a comma and you will need to invert the subject and verb in the main clause.

infinitive clause ⎸ main clause
*Ohne etwas zu sagen, ⎸ **verließ sie** das Haus.*

Notice that we are using the 'verb–comma–verb' pattern.

rufen die Haustür alles das Hemd verschwenden abschließen fernsehen verstehen zu viel

1 Link the sentences with the subordinating conjunction given in brackets.

Example: Ich rufe dich an. Ich bin in Regensburg angekommen. (**sobald**)
→ *Ich rufe dich an, **sobald** ich in Regensburg angekommen bin.*

a Ich habe eine Stunde gewartet. Sie ist nach Hause gekommen. (**bis**)

_____

b Sie können mich einfach anrufen. Es gibt Probleme. (**falls**)

_____

c Der Skateboardfahrer brach den Weltrekord. Er sprang über eine 25 Meter lange Grube. (**indem**)

_____

d Meine Freundinnen treiben nicht genug Sport. Sie wollen fit werden. (**obwohl**)

_____

2 Rewrite your answers to Exercise 1 so that they start with the subordinate clause.

Example: Ich rufe dich an, sobald ich in Regensburg angekommen bin.
→ *Sobald ich in Regensburg angekommen bin, rufe ich dich an.*

a _____

b _____

c _____

d _____

3 Translate these sentence completions into German, using the words below to help you.

a Wir wohnen in einem Wohnwagen, _____

_____.
(*since we sold our house*)

b Er kam nach Hause, _____.
(*as soon as school finished*)

c Was macht die Regierung, _____

_____?
(*so that people stay healthy*)

d _____,
wird der Lehrer bestimmt helfen.
(*In case you [fam. sing.] have [any] difficulties*)

e Sein Sohn ist zufrieden, _____.
(*as long as he is allowed to use the computer*)

f _____,
muss mein Bruder immer das neueste Modell haben.
(*Although his mobile phone is not very old*)

Grammatik

We looked at **subordinate clauses** and **subordinating conjunctions** on page 13. A subordinate clause does not usually stand on its own, but goes either before or after the main clause in the sentence.

You can recognise the subordinate clause because it will start with a subordinating conjunction such as *weil* or *wenn*, which will make the **finite verb** go to the end of that clause:

[main clause]
Er möchte Golfprofi werden,

[subordinate clause]
wenn er älter **ist.**

subordinating conjunctions	
bis	until
damit	in order that, so that (= intention)
falls	in case
indem	by (doing)
obwohl	although
obgleich	although
sobald	as soon as
so dass	so that (= with the result that)
solange	as long as
seit	since
seitdem	since
wenn	when
weil	because

das Haus
nutzen
die Schule
Schwierigkeiten
der Computer
Menschen
aus
gesund
verkaufen

FIRSTPIECESFOR
CLASSICALGUITAR

Master Twenty Beautiful Classical Guitar Studies

ROBTHORPE

FUNDAMENTALCHANGES

First Pieces for Classical Guitar

Published by **www.fundamental-changes.com**

ISBN: 978-1-911267-80-5

www.fundamental-changes.com

Cover Image Copyright: ShutterStock Minerva Studio

Contents

Foreword

This book was inspired by students who had the passion and ability to learn classical guitar, but felt held back either by starting later in life or not reading music.

Guitarists often get bogged down in the details of theory and technique. They learn licks or short extracts from songs, while secretly dreading the moment when someone says, "Well, go on, play something!" Developing the mechanics of playing guitar is important, but it should always be done in support of playing music. This is where repertoire building comes in. Having whole pieces under your belt (even short ones) is rewarding. It will help you to make sense of the nuts and bolts of theory, and allow you to share your music with family and friends.

Learning to read musical notation is a worthwhile skill to develop, as it allows you to learn music written for other instruments, communicate ideas with other instrumentalists, and is essential for most professional jobs in the industry. However, I strongly feel that students whose goal is to simply play guitar for their own pleasure should be able to access music they want to play without the need to develop the skill to read complex musical notation.

This collection of classical pieces will make up a satisfying performance repertoire for the advancing beginner while developing your technique as you work through progressively more challenging pieces.

The music is drawn from some of the most famous and influential composers for the guitar, including Carulli, Giuliani, Carcassi, and Fernando Sor. In addition, it dips into acoustic guitar music with traditional folk tune arrangements.

The commentary for each piece discusses some of the technical challenges, but this book is intended primarily as a collection of music. I suggest you use it in conjunction with a dedicated technique method book or a local teacher.

I hope these pieces prove helpful and inspire you to explore the music for guitar that has been written over the past four centuries, as well as encouraging you to write some arrangements of your own.

Good luck!

Rob

1 Complete the sentences with the imperfect subjunctive of the verbs given in brackets.

a Wenn ich nicht so faul _____ , _____ ich öfter schwimmen gehen. (**sein, werden**)

b Wo _____ du wohnen, wenn du viel Geld _____? (**werden, haben**)

c Ich _____ in die Bibliothek gehen, wenn es dort eine bessere

Auswahl an Büchern _____. (**werden, geben**)

d Wenn es kein Erdöl oder Erdgas mehr _____ , was _____ wir dann machen? (**geben, werden**)

e Mein Vater _____ mir helfen, wenn er es nicht so eilig _____. (**werden, haben**)

f Wenn ich ein Auto _____ , _____ ich selbständiger sein. (**haben, können**)

g Es _____ toll, wenn meine Mutter mehr Geduld mit mir

_____. (**sein, haben**)

h Wenn seine Freunde ihn nicht besuchen _____ , _____ er sehr enttäuscht. (**dürfen, sein**)

2 Complete these conditional sentences with your own ideas.

a Wenn ich mehr Zeit hätte, _____

_____

b Wenn es keine illegalen Drogen mehr gäbe, _____

_____

c Wenn er schlanker wäre, _____

_____

d Wenn ich reich wäre, _____

_____

3 Translate these phrases into German, using the verbs in the margin.

a She would have bought _____ .

b They would have been _____ .

c We would have stayed _____ .

d My parents would have rung _____ .

e I would have written _____ .

f He would have gone away _____ .

g Would you (*fam. sg.*) have asked? _____ .

h We would have arrived _____ .

Grammatik

As we saw with modal verbs, the **imperfect subjunctive** can be used to convey the idea of 'would'. You are already familiar with *würde* meaning 'would' when using the conditional (it is actually the imperfect subjunctive form of *werden*).

Notice that *würde … haben, würde … sein* and *würde … geben* are often abbreviated to *hätte, wäre* and *gäbe*.

You use the imperfect subjunctive in conditional clauses with *wenn* if you wish to say the following:

If I had … *Wenn ich … hätte …*
If I were … *Wenn ich … wäre …*
If there were … *Wenn es … gäbe …*

In a sentence, it would look like this:

Wenn ich steinreich wäre, würde ich mir einen Ferrari kaufen. If I were very rich, I would buy myself a Ferrari.

Add the same endings to *hätte, wäre* and *gäbe* as shown for *würde*:

ich würde
du würdest
er/sie/es würde
wir würden
ihr würdet
Sie/sie würden

Grammatik

When used with a past participle, the forms *hätte* and *wäre* can also be used as part of a tense called the **pluperfect subjunctive** (also known as the **conditional perfect**) which is used to express 'would have done'.

*Sie **hätte** mehr Freunde **eingeladen**, wenn …* She **would have invited** more friends if …
N.B. *einladen* is used with the auxiliary *haben*.

*Wir **wären** früher **abgefahren**, wenn …* We **would have set off** earlier if …
N.B. *abfahren* is used with the auxiliary *sein*.

| fragen anrufen bleiben |
| ankommen sein weggehen |
| kaufen schreiben |

Topic 3: Relative pronouns

1 Choose the correct form of the relative pronoun. Then translate the sentences into English.

a Das ist der Gürtel, **der / den / das** sie gestern gekauft hat.

_____

b Der Fußballspieler, **der / dessen / das** Arm gebrochen wurde, musste ins Krankenhaus.

_____

c Sie hat einen Ring gefunden, **der / den / die** sehr wertvoll ist.

_____

d Die Leute, **der / deren / die** neben uns wohnen, sind sehr freundlich.

_____

e Die Dame, mit **die / der / den** ich gesprochen habe, ist meine ehemalige Englischlehrerin.

_____

f Alkohol ist eine Droge, **die / der / denen** oft missbraucht wird.

_____

2 Translate these sentences into German. Use the words in the box at the bottom to help you.

a The film (which) we saw last week was excellent.

_____

b The boy whose bike was stolen was really angry.

_____

c The houses in which the people were living were dilapidated.

_____

d She has recently married the man she met in Spain last year.

_____

e The sofa the dog was lying on is dirty now.

_____

f The garden we were sitting in had a pond.

_____

3 Complete these sentences with information which is relevant for you personally.

a Ich habe einen Freund / eine Freundin, der /die_____

_____ .

b Vor kurzem habe ich ein Lied gehört, das _____

_____ .

c Wir wohnen in einem Dorf / in einer Stadt, das / die _____

_____ .

Grammatik

A **relative clause** is a subordinate clause containing a **relative pronoun** which usually refers back to a noun in the preceding clause. Relative pronouns in English are 'who(m)', 'whose', 'which' and 'that'.

In German, relative pronouns are similar to the word for 'the', but there are some exceptions:

	masc.	fem.	neuter	plural
nom.	der	die	das	die
acc.	den	die	das	die
gen.	dessen	deren	dessen	deren
dat.	dem	der	dem	denen

The relative pronoun takes its number and gender from the noun it refers to, but it gets its case from its function in the relative clause:

Er kennt | einen Mann, | der | Drogen nimmt. He knows a man who takes drugs.

Here _Mann_ is the direct object (accusative) of _kennt_, but _der_ is the subject (nominative) of _nimmt_.

The relative clause is separated from the main clause by a comma.

Tipp

Be careful to use the correct words for 'who' and 'which'. If they are question words, use _wer_ and _welch-_ etc., <u>not</u> relative pronouns.

Tipp

In English we often miss out the relative pronoun, i.e. we drop 'which/that' from this sentence:

The apple (which/that) I ate this morning wasn't sweet.

In German it **must** be included:

Der Apfel, **den** ich heute Morgen gegessen habe, war nicht süß.

das Sofa	schmutzig
der Garten	das Fahrrad
verfallen (adj.)	böse
der Teich	der Film
jetzt	enthalten
ausgezeichnet	heiraten
liegen	vor kurzem

1 Circle the appropriate form of the imperative according to the person being spoken to (as stated in brackets).

   a **Komm / Kommt / Kommen Sie** eine Stunde später! (*you are speaking to two friends*)

   b **Warte / Wartet / Warten Sie** einen Augenblick, bitte! (*shop assistant to adult customer*)

   c **Setz dich / Setzt euch / Setzen Sie** sich hin! (*teacher to pupil*)

   d **Bring / Bringt / Bringen Sie** mir eine Tasse Kaffee, bitte! (*guest to waiter*)

   e **Sei / Seid / Seien Sie** ruhig! (*owner to dogs*)

   f **Mach / Macht / Machen Sie** das Fenster zu, bitte! (*you to a friend*)

2 Give the three imperative forms of these verbs.

   a bleiben → _____ _____

   _____

   b antworten → _____ _____

   _____

   c sich waschen → _____ _____

   _____

   d nehmen → _____ _____

   _____

3 Translate these instructions or commands into German. Use the words in the box to help you.

   a Ring me at 6 o'clock. (*you to a friend*)

   _____

   b Take the tablets now. (*doctor to adult patient*)

   _____

   c Switch off the computer. (*mother to children*)

   _____

   d Read the magazine. (*you to a friend*)

   _____

   e Tidy your room. (*father to daughter*)

   _____

Grammatik

The **imperative** form of the verb is used for telling someone to do something. Depending on who is being spoken to, there are three different forms, based on the different words for 'you' and using the present tense. An exclamation mark used at the end of the sentence can give more emphasis.

The *du* form

Take the *du* form of the verb and miss off the ending *-st*:

kommen → du kommst → Komm!

arbeiten → du arbeitest → Arbeite!

sehen → du siehst → Sieh!

aufpassen → du passt auf → Pass auf!

If the *du* form has the letter *ä* but the infinitive has **a** (no umlaut), the imperative must also have *a*:

lassen → du lässt → Lass!

The *ihr* form

Take the *ihr* form of the verb and simply miss out *ihr*:

bringen → ihr bringt → Bringt!

The *Sie* form

Take the *Sie* form of the verb and just put *Sie* afterwards:

gehen → Sie gehen → Gehen Sie!

Tipp

With reflexive verbs, place the appropriate reflexive pronoun after the verb:

sich setzen → Setz dich! Setzt euch! Setzen Sie sich!

sich vorstellen → Stell dir vor! Stellt euch vor! Stellen Sie sich vor!

Tipp

The imperative forms of *sein* need to be learned by heart:

sein → Sei! Seid! Seien Sie!

| ausschalten | die Zeitschrift | aufräumen | nehmen | lesen | jetzt | anrufen | der Computer |

1 Circle the correct form of the adjectival noun in each sentence.

a **Der Obdachlose / Den Obdachlosen / Die Obdachlosen** schläft unter der Eisenbahnbrücke. (*homeless man*)

b Die Kinder haben mit **eine Erwachsene / einer Erwachsenen / einem Erwachsenen** gesprochen. (*adult woman*)

c Man muss versuchen, **die Armen / dem Armen / den Armen** der Welt zu helfen. (*poor people*)

d Die Sanitäter versuchten, **der Drogensüchtigen / die Drogensüchtige / der Drogensüchtige** das Leben zu retten. (*female drug addict*)

e **Der Blinden / Die Blinden / Die Blinde** wohnt ganz allein. (*blind woman*)

f Er hat viele **Bekannter / Bekannte / Bekannten**, aber fast keine Freunde. (*acquaintances*)

g Hier gibt es nicht genug Parkplätze für **Behinderte / Behinderten / Behinderter**. (*disabled people*)

h Wir durften nicht mit **den Gefangenen / der Gefangenen / dem Gefangenen** sprechen. (*male prisoner*)

2 Complete the sentences with the correct adjectival noun. Use the words in the box on the right to help you

a (*A German woman*) _____ wurde gestern bei einem Unfall schwer verletzt.

b Die alkoholischen Getränke waren nur für _____ (*the adults*).

c Die Ärztin gab _____ (*a sick woman*) eine Spritze.

d Heute Nachmittag gehe ich mit _____ (*a male relative*) ins Café.

e An der Straßenecke stand _____ (*a blind man*) mit seinem Hund.

f Im Stadtzentrum hat _____ (*a homeless woman*) um Geld gebettelt.

g Der Abenteuerpark hat _____ (*the young people*) sehr gut gefallen.

h (*A disabled man*) _____ saß im Rollstuhl.

3 Complete the sentences with the correct adjectival noun.

a _____ daran war, dass es kostenlos war. (*the good thing*)

b Was war _____, was du je gemacht hast? (*the worst thing*)

c _____ in seinem Leben ist sein Auto. (*the most important thing*)

d Zum Glück war _____ des Gebäudes nicht beschädigt. (*the interior*)

Grammatik

Adjectives can be used as **adjectival nouns**. They have the appropriate adjectival ending (see pages 55–56) and, like a noun, start with a capital letter.

der alte Mann → der Alte – the old man

die alte Frau → die Alte – the old woman

ein alter Mann → ein Alter – an old man

eine alte Frau → eine Alte – an old woman

die alten Leute → die Alten – the old people

Ich kenne einen Drogensüchtigen. I know a (male) drug addict.

Der Reporter hat mit der Obdachlosen gesprochen. The reporter has spoken to the homeless woman.

Er hat ein Foto eines Obdachlosen gemacht. He took a photo of a homeless man.

Es gab keinen Platz mehr für die Kranken. There was no more space for the sick people.

Das Hotel ist nur für Erwachsene. The hotel is for adults only.

Viele Obdachlose schlafen auf den Straßen. Many homeless people sleep on the streets.

Tipp

Adjectival nouns can refer to things as well as people and are always neuter, e.g. *das Schöne, das Äußere* (exterior), *das Beste* (best thing), *das Interessanteste* (most interesting thing).

---

krank jugendlich behindert
deutsch verwandt obdachlos
erwachsen blind

---

wichtig inner schlimm gut

1 Complete these half-sentences with an appropriate imperfect subjunctive form chosen from those in the box beneath *Grammatik*. Which word in the box is not used?

Example: a *Wenn ich ein schnelleres Auto <u>hätte</u>, …*

b Wenn euer Zug nicht pünktlich _____ , …

c Wenn sie nicht so schüchtern _____ , …

d Wenn du nicht so ungeduldig _____ , …

e Wenn unsere Freundinnen nicht mitkommen _____ , …

f Wenn ich beim Abspülen helfen _____ , …

g Wenn es keine Markenkleidung _____ ,…

    Not used: _____

2 Complete these sentences in the conditional (*würde* + ending, as appropriate).

i Ich _____ nicht so viel Geld ausgeben.

ii Ihr _____ den Anschlusszug verpassen.

iii Ich __<u>würde</u>__ meine Freunde bestimmt beeindrucken.

iv Wir _____ enttäuscht sein.

v Meine Schwestern _____ mehr Freunde kennen lernen.

vi Es _____ mir egal sein.

vii Du _____ eine nette Person sein.

3 Join the sentences in Exercise 2 to the sentence halves in Exercise 1 so that they make sense. Be careful to use the correct word order.

    Example: a *Wenn ich ein schnelleres Auto hätte, würde ich meine Freunde bestimmt beeindrucken.*

    _____

    _____

    _____

    _____

    _____

    _____

4 Complete these sentences with a *wenn*-clause of your own, using a different imperfect subjunctive form each time.

a Ich würde mich freuen, wenn _____

    _____ .

b Meine Eltern würden es hassen, wenn _____

    _____ .

c Meine Freunde würden mich auslachen, wenn _____

    _____

Grammatik

We looked at how to form and use the imperfect subjunctive on page 41. A **conditional sentence** can express the idea of 'if something were to happen, something else would happen'. The conditional or the imperfect subjunctive must then be used in both parts of the sentence, e.g.

*Ich **würde** ein schönes Haus **kaufen**, wenn ich reich **wäre**.* I would buy a beautiful house if I were rich.

*Wenn wir Zeit **hätten**, **könnten** wir das Schloss **besichtigen**.* If we had time, we could visit the castle.

As well as knowing the key words **wäre**, **hätte** and **gäbe** to use in *wenn*-clauses, remember that the imperfect subjunctive form of modal verbs will also be useful (see page 38).

Other useful verbs are *käme* (from *kommen*), and **wüsste** (from *wissen*).

dürften gäbe wären <u>hätte</u>
wärest müsste wüsste käme

Tipp

If the sentence starts with the **subordinate clause**, remember to invert the subject and verb in the **main clause**.

Grammatik

Particles are words which usually give emphasis in a sentence. They are not always easy to translate into English, where there might be a change in intonation to convey the desired meaning.

doch

This can be used to persuade the listener of the speaker's point of view or show some disagreement:

Gestern hat es doch geregnet. It rained yesterday, didn't it?

Er hat es doch gesagt. He said it all the same.

It can be used in commands to give a sense of urgency:

Lass mich doch rein! Do let me in!

ja

Can express surprise in a statement:

Das ist ja unerhört. That really is outrageous.

Otherwise it can express the speaker's insistence that s/he is correct:

Wir sind ja gestern ins Restaurant gegangen. We **did** go to the restaurant yesterday.

mal

Can be used for 'just' and is often used in commands, requests and questions:

Guck mal! (Just) look!

schon

Can be used to express agreement with some reservation:

Das ist schon möglich. That is quite possible, but …

It can add insistence to a command:

Komm schon! (Do) come on!

or reassurance that something will happen:

Es wird schon gehen. It'll be OK (don't worry about it).

---

1 Choose an appropriate particle to fit in these sentences..

a Hör _____ zu! (*Just listen.*)

b Das ist _____ Blödsinn! (*That's really stupid!*)

c Mach _____! (*Get a move on!*)

d Ich habe es dir _____ gesagt! (*I did tell you!*)

e Pass _____ auf! (*Do mind what you are doing!*)

f Wir werden es _____ schaffen! (*We'll do/make it, I assure you.*)

g Hör _____ endlich auf! (*Stop it, will you!*)

h Moment _____! (*Just a moment!*)

i Man weiß _____ nie! (*You never know!*)

j Das kann _____ sein. (*That may well be.*)

1 Circle the correct time phrase in each sentence.

a **Einen Tag / Eines Tages** werden wir zurückkommen.

b Letzten Monat bin ich **vier Tage / für vier Tage** auf diesem Campingplatz geblieben.

c Meine Familie und ich sind schon **eine Woche / vor einer Woche** hier.

d Sein Freund wohnt **seit einem Jahr / für ein Jahr** in Hannover. (*has been living*)

e Mein Bruder möchte **einen Morgen / eines Morgens** einen langen Spaziergang machen.

f **Vor drei Jahren / Für drei Jahre** haben wir zehn Tage auf Mallorca verbracht.

g Wir kennen uns schon fast **sechs Monate / vor sechs Monaten.**

h Nächsten Sommer möchte ich **für zehn Tage / seit zehn Tagen** eine Radtour durch die Niederlande machen.

2 Translate the following phrases into German.

a after a week _____

b in two hours _____

c during the spring _____

d at midnight _____

e on Friday _____

f in the evening _____

g at Easter _____

h one night _____

i until next Wednesday _____

j one year ago _____

k before the trip _____

l since last week _____

m about 10 o'clock _____

n on 3rd May _____

Grammatik

- Use the accusative for time phrases without a preposition and referring to a definite time period (see page 9):

Wir sind nur einen Tag in Luxemburg geblieben.

- Use the genitive case when referring to an indefinite time period (see page 29):

Hoffentlich wird sie eines Tages heiraten.

- Translate 'for' with *für* only if it refers to a future time, although it is not always necessary to include it:

*Nächstes Jahr werden wir (**für**) zwei Wochen bleiben.*

Letztes Jahr sind wir nur eine Woche geblieben.

- When referring to a time which started in the past and is still going on, use *seit* + dative (see pages 22 and 35):

*Sie lernt **seit** einem Jahr Deutsch.*

(*schon* + accusative is an alternative)

- Time phrases can be used with other prepositions such as *an, bis, gegen, in, nach, um, während, vor* and *zu* (see pages 9–10, 29).

Tipp

Remember that *vor* + dative means **'ago'**, NOT 'for'! Also don't forget that *seit* is used with the **present tense,** e.g.

*Seit drei Monaten **wohnen** wir auf dem Land.* We have been living in the country for three months.

1 Identify the different verb forms in the following sentences. Put a circle round the verbs in the subjunctive, underline the verbs in the imperative and mark infinitive forms with a cross.

a Was würdest du machen, wenn du kein Handy hättest?

b Ohne ein einziges Wort zu sagen, hat sie das Zimmer verlassen.

c Kommen Sie morgen vorbei, wenn Sie Zeit haben.

d Anstatt eine SMS zu schicken, hat er eine E-Mail geschickt.

e Wir wären ins Konzert gegangen, wenn wir Karten gehabt hätten.

f Bleib hier, wenn du willst.

g Wir wollen ins Kino gehen, um den neuesten Actionfilm zu sehen.

h Seid doch ruhig!

2 Which modal verb is suitable? Underline the correct word.

a Vielleicht **könnten / konnten** wir nächstes Jahr ein preiswertes Hotel im Internet finden.

b Ich **müsste / musste** früh aufstehen, weil ich das Auto waschen wollte.

c Um gesund zu bleiben, **möchten / mochten** wir in der Zukunft öfter joggen gehen.

d Obwohl sie es sich damals leisten **könnte / konnte**, wollte sie das Kleid nicht kaufen.

e Wenn es nicht so teuer wäre, **könntest / konntest** du nach Asien fliegen.

f Ihre Freundin **dürfte / durfte** nicht mitgehen, weil sie nicht alt genug war.

g Als mein Freund jünger war, **könnte / konnte** er den Geschmack von Spinat nicht leiden.

h Wenn meine Schwester älter wäre, **dürfte / durfte** sie allein in Urlaub fahren.

3 Complete the following sentences with the correct relative pronouns.

a Ich habe einen Freund, _____ immer hilfsbereit ist.

b Er kennt die Frau nicht, _____ er das Paket geben soll.

c Der Mann, _____ wir vor kurzem kennen lernten, ist leider gestorben.

d Das war die beste Wohnung, in _____ wir je übernachtet haben.

e Die Drogen, _____ er auf der Straße fand, waren illegal.

f Der Tag, an _____ sie heirateten, war sehr schön.

g Das ist das Motorrad, _____ ich am Montag gekauft habe.

h Die Schülerin, _____ Eltern in Neuseeland wohnen, hat manchmal Heimweh.

4a Read the text. Then read the statements. Write T, if the statement is true, F if the statement is false, or NA if the information doesn't appear in the text.

Wann wurde eigentlich die Fernsehfernbedienung erfunden? Das ist lange her. Die Fernbedienung* gab es Mitte der 50er Jahre ohne Kabel. Da der DVD-Spieler, der Videorekorder und der Satellitenempfänger eine eigene Fernbedienung haben müssen, ist inzwischen das ganze Wohnzimmer voll damit. Und der Fernseher wird immer schlauer*: Man kann Fotos anschauen, spielen oder im Internet surfen.

Weil man mit der Fernbedienung keine Internetadresse schreiben kann, sind die Tage der Fernbedienung gezählt. Und wie sollen wir in Zukunft den Fernseher bedienen? Indem wir mit ihm reden und ihm Zeichen geben. Anfang des Jahres wurde auf der weltweit größten Messe* für Unterhaltungselektronik in Las Vegas ein solcher Fernseher vorgestellt – mit Sprach- und Gestenbedienung*.

Der neue Fernseher hat Augen und Ohren oberhalb des Bildschirms. Kamera und Mikrofon können uns sehen und hören. Statt den Fernseher einzuschalten, reicht einfach eine Begrüßung, z. B. „'n Abend Fernseher". Wenn man das Programm wechseln will, genügt ein „Kanal wechseln, Kanal 4". Und falls man keine Lust hat, mit dem Fernseher zu reden, reicht auch eine Handbewegung.

Wann gibt es diesen neuen Fernseher zu kaufen? Ab Ende März. Der Preis liegt zwischen 1500 € und 3000 €, je nach Größe. Nur eins ist übrigens unklar: Wie soll der Fernseher meine Gesten im Dunkeln sehen? Dann kann man ja mit ihm reden!

* Fernbedienung – *remote control*
schlau – *cunning, clever, crafty*
die Messe – *fair*
die Gestenbedienung – *motion control*

a   Die Fernsehfernbedienung wurde im zwanzigsten Jahrhundert erfunden.　□

b   Es gibt normalerweise eine einzelne Fernbedienung für alle Geräte.　□

c   Mit dem zukünftigen Fernseher wird man keine Fernbedienung brauchen.　□

d   Der Fernseher der Zukunft kann verschiedene Sprachen verstehen.　□

e   Mit einer Kombination aus Gesten- und Sprachsteuerung soll man den Fernseher bedienen können.　□

f   Diesen Fernseher kann man zum ersten Mal im Herbst kaufen.　□

4b Now put a circle round the modal verbs in the text and underline the subordinate clauses.

1a Lesen Sie die folgenden Äußerungen über Schönheit. Schreiben Sie dann den passenden Namen (Andreas, Katharina, Daniela, Timo, Jennifer, Sebastian) zu jeder Aussage.

Meinung: Ist Schönheit wichtig?

Um wie die Stars auszusehen, muss man sehr viel bezahlen. Ich finde, dass jeder so aussehen sollte, wie es ihm gefällt. Wer so wie die Stars aus dem Fernsehen aussehen will, kann das ruhig machen. **Andreas**

Schönheit, was ist das genau? Farben können schön sein oder auch ein Auto. Ein Gesicht oder ein Körper kann auch schön sein. Die Schönheit liegt im Auge des Betrachters. Es gibt immer welche, die etwas schön finden. **Katharina**

Je attraktiver ein Gesicht, desto sympathischer, fleißiger, intelligenter und erfolgreicher die Person. **Daniela**

Kommt Schönheit nicht von innen heraus? Die meisten Leute tun etwas, um für andere attraktiv auszusehen oder um sich einfach besser zu fühlen. Jedes Geschlecht tut was für die Schönheit, um nach außen gut rüberzukommen. **Timo**

Viele Leute denken, dass hübsche Menschen auch gleich intelligent sind. Aber die Intelligenz hat mit dem Erscheinungsbild nichts zu tun. Um intelligent zu sein, ist ein schönes Gesicht nicht unbedingt notwendig. **Jennifer**

Schönheit hilft, stimmt das wirklich? Natürlich ist es anfangs gut, wenn der Chef bei einer Bewerbung sieht, dass man „schön" ist. Aber bessere Chancen hat man dadurch in den meisten Berufen nicht. Um erfolgreich zu sein, braucht man gute Zeugnisse. **Sebastian**

a _____ meint, sowohl Männer als Frauen versuchen, sich schöner zu machen.

b _____ glaubt, man kann intelligent sein, ohne besonders attraktiv zu wirken.

c _____ meint, dass Schönheit ihren Preis hat.

d _____ will eher auf die Qualifikationen als auf das Aussehen achten.

e _____ ist der Meinung, dass es viele Arten von Schönheit gibt.

f _____ glaubt, dass man auch andere gute Eigenschaften hat, wenn man schön aussieht.

1b Lesen Sie den Text noch einmal und unterstreichen Sie alle Satzteile mit ‚um … zu'.

1c Lesen Sie die Meinung von Manuela. Sie müssen aber den letzten Satz in die richtige Reihenfolge bringen.

Ich finde mich ohne Make-up hässlich. Ohne Schminke kann ich das Haus nicht verlassen.

Arbeit – um – ich – eine – für – Stunde – machen – mich – zu – brauche – fertig – die – mindestens

(*I need at least an hour to get ready for work.*)

_____

_____

Manuela

2 Ergänzen Sie die folgenden Sätze mit der richtigen Verbform.

a Kennst du die Familie, die jetzt neben uns _____? (**wohnen**)

b Wenn ich die Gelegenheit _____ , würde ich Fallschirmspringen ausprobieren.   (**haben**)

c Weil ich eine Beinverletzung hatte, _____ ich drei Wochen lang nicht trainieren. (**dürfen**)

d Immer mehr Designerdrogen werden heutzutage _____. (**produzieren**)

e Weil mein Hund krank war, _____ wir den Tierarzt anrufen. (**müssen**)

f Vati, _____ nicht so viele Kartoffelchips, weil sie viel Fett enthalten! (**essen**)

g Wenn es möglich wäre, _____ wir früher kommen. (**werden**)

h Da es so spannend aussah, _____ ich Wakeboarding lernen. (**wollen**)

i Meine Freunde _____ nicht gekommen, wenn sie das gewusst _____. (**sein**, **haben**)

j Ich _____ ein anderes Hotel empfehlen, wenn mein Aufenthalt hier unbefriedigend wäre. (**müssen**)

3 Ergänzen Sie die folgenden Sätze mit den richtigen Fallendungen.

a Es gibt immer noch zu viel__ Arm__ auf der Welt.

b D__ Gefangen__ mussten fast den ganzen Tag in ihren Zellen verbringen.

c Er hat d__ Obdachlos__ ein paar Euro gegeben. (*homeless woman*)

d Ein__ Verwandt__ von ihm lebt noch in den USA. (*male*)

e Ich habe gerade mit ein__Bekannt__ gesprochen. (*male*)

f D__ Drogensüchtig__ verschwendet ihr Geld und ihr Leben. (*female*)

g Wir kennen d__ Jugendlich__ nicht. (*people*)

h Kinderkrankheiten bei Erwachsen__ können manchmal gefährlich sein.

i Sein__ Verlobt__ wollte ihn am Abend vor der Hochzeit nicht sehen. (*female*)

j Beim Flugzeugabsturz gab es überhaupt kein__ Überlebend__ . (*survivors*)

Topic 4: Infinitives

1 What do these abbreviations stand for? Make sure you know what they mean. Give an example of each verb type.

a vi _____ Example: _____

b sep _____ _____

c vt _____ _____

d irreg _____ _____

e vr _____ _____

f insep _____ _____

g aux _____ _____

Grammatik

Remember that the verb or phrase which you find in the dictionary is just your starting point because the verb ending is likely to need changing, cases might need to be used, word order might need to be changed, and so on.

Tipp

Grammatical terminology is often shortened in a dictionary to save space, but make sure that you know what the abbreviations stand for by checking the list given elsewhere in the dictionary.

2 Using the following verbs and phrases from a dictionary, write notes about what the abbreviations mean. Then translate the sentences into German.

Example: **sich bei jdm für etw bedanken** *vr* to say thank you to s.o. for sth

Notes: *reflexive verb, **to** somebody = **bei** + dative, **for** something = **für** etwas*

I thank him for the present. Ich bedanke mich bei ihm für das Geschenk.

a **untersuchen** *vt insep* to examine

Notes: _____

The doctor examines me.

_____

Tipp

Always pay attention to small details, e.g.

jdn auslachen = jemanden (acc.) auslachen to laugh at someone

e.g. *Sie haben mich ausgelacht.* They laughed at me.

jdm etw verdanken = jemandem (dat.) etwas verdanken to owe something to somebody

e.g. *Er verdankt mir viel.* He owes me a lot.

b **jdm/einer Sache widersprechen** *insep vi* to contradict s.o./sth

Notes: _____

They always contradict him.

_____

c **etw als selbstverständlich hinnehmen** *vt sep irreg* to take something for granted

Notes: _____

You (fam. sg.) take it for granted.

_____

d **jdm etw beibringen** *vt sep irreg* to teach s.o. sth

Notes: _____

He is teaching you (fam. pl.) Italian.

_____

e **jdm etw vergeben** *irreg vt* to forgive s.o. (for) sth

Notes: _____

I shall forgive you (fam. sg.) for the accident (der Unfall).

_____

f **jdn überfahren** *vt insep* to knock down, run over s.o.

Notes: _____

The lorry ran him over.

_____

g **entgegenlaufen** *vi sep aux sein + dat* to run towards

Notes: _____

She ran towards me.

_____

h **umziehen** *sep irreg vr* to get changed

Notes: _____

They got changed quickly.

_____

i **sich von jdm verabschieden** *vr* to say goodbye to s.o.

Notes: _____

We said goodbye to our friends.

_____

j **bei jdm den Eindruck erwecken** *vt* to give s.o. the impression

Notes: _____

She gave her the impression that ...

_____

1 Choose the correct form of the possessive adjective.

a Warst du gerade bei **deine / deiner / dein** Freundin?

b Um wie viel Uhr kommen **eure / euer / euren** Verwandten an?

c Ich habe **meine / meiner / meinen** Eltern ein Foto von **mein / meinem / meiner** Freund gezeigt.

d Wegen **seiner / seine / seinem** Verletzungen wollte **ihre / ihr / ihren** Onkel niemanden sehen.

e Sie ist sofort ausgegangen, ohne **ihr / ihren / ihre** E-Mails zu lesen.

f Am Anfang **unserer / unseren / unsere** Schulferien sind wir nach Portugal geflogen.

2 Translate the phrases into German, using the words in the box to help you. Check cases after prepositions (see pages 22–23).

a in my life _____

b for his uncle _____

c after our break _____

d during their stay _____

e from your (fam.sg.) sister _____

f opposite their house _____

g instead of her pen _____

h without his camera _____

i with your (pol.) dogs _____

j since her accident _____

3 Complete the sentences with endings as appropriate.

a Mein____ Vater kennt die Chefin dein____ Mutter.

b Auf mein____ Tisch lagen mein____ Handy und mein____ Portemonnaie.

c Gib dein____ Vati sein____ Brille!

d Sein____ Eltern haben schon mit sein____ Lehrerin gesprochen.

e Mein____ Kamm kann ich einfach nicht finden.

f Sie hat ihr____ Freund sein____ Fotos zurückgegeben.

g Wir haben den Hochzeitstag unser____Eltern gefeiert.

h In eur____ Garten gibt es viele Blumen.

i Ich habe mein____ Tante ein Geschenk zum Geburtstag geschickt.

j Nach Ihr____ langen Reise müssen Sie erschöpft sein!

Grammatik

We first looked at possessive adjectives and the endings they use on page 32. Here is some further practice.

Tipp

Take care with the word *ihr* and its different meanings. Don't get mixed up between using it as a possessive adjective and using it as a pronoun. Remember that *ihr* is likely to have an ending on it if it is being used as a possessive adjective, but will never have one if it is a pronoun.

Tipp

When deciding on the endings to use with *sein* (his) and *ihr* (her/their), remember that it has nothing to do with the gender of the people being referred to. The endings are based on the gender, number and case of the following noun.

seine Tochter – feminine ending (*-e*) because *Tochter* is feminine.

ihr Bruder – masculine ending because *Bruder* is masculine.

der Fotoapparat die Pause

der Unfall der Kuli das Leben

der Hund der Aufenthalt

Topic 4: The pluperfect tense

1 Complete the sentences with the correct form of *haben* or *sein*, as appropriate. Then translate into English.

a Zum Glück _____ wir den Bus nicht verpasst.

_____

b Ich _____ entschieden, den Erste-Hilfe-Kurs zu machen.

_____

c Brigitte _____ im See schwimmen gegangen, obgleich das Wetter sehr kalt war.

_____

d Es _____ angefangen zu schneien, aber das war uns egal.

_____

e Ich _____ gerade ins Bett gegangen, als das Telefon klingelte.

_____

2 Complete the sentences with the pluperfect tense of the verbs given in brackets.

a Nachdem er den Brief _____ _____, rief er mich an. (**lesen**)

b Nach der Überfahrt _____ ich mich krank _____. (**fühlen**)

c Meine Freundin _____ noch nie im Ausland _____, also machten wir einen Tagesausflug nach Frankreich. (**sein**)

d Nach den Examen _____ meine Freunde in Urlaub _____. (**fahren**)

e Ich _____ _____ , sie anzurufen, aber leider _____ sie das Haus schon _____ (**versuchen, verlassen**)

f Bevor meine Familie und ich nach Deutschland kamen, _____ meine Oma leider _____ (**sterben**)

g Da es viel kälter _____ _____, wollten wir nicht ausgehen. (**werden**)

3 Translate the following sentences into English.

a Das Haus war durch eine Explosion beschädigt worden.

_____

b Leider waren die Juwelen nie gefunden worden.

_____

c Vor 100 Jahren war das Mobiltelefon noch nicht erfunden worden.

_____

Grammatik

By now, you should know the perfect tense and how to form it, so using the **pluperfect tense** is really easy. Use it for things which had happened. To form it, instead of using the present tense of the auxiliary verbs *haben/sein* + past participle, you use the **imperfect tense** of those same verbs (*hatte/war*) + past participle:

*Nachdem er seinem Vater im Garten **geholfen hatte**, spielte er Gitarre.* After he **had helped** his father in the garden, he played the guitar.

*Meine Oma hat einen Laptop gekauft, weil ihr alter Computer **kaputtgegangen war***. My gran bought a laptop because her old computer **had broken**.

Tipp

Always read the whole sentence when trying to work out the meaning. Don't be tempted into thinking that *war* + past participle means 'was doing'. It always means 'had done'.

Grammatik

The pluperfect passive

In the **passive** (see pages 20–21), the pluperfect tense is formed from the imperfect tense of *sein* + past participle + *worden*.

*Ihr Auto **war gestohlen worden***. Her car had been stolen.

*Brücken **waren** zwischen den Generationen **gebaut worden***. Bridges **had been built** between the generations.

Compare that with the **perfect passive**, which uses the present tense of *sein* + past participle + *worden*.

*Ihr Auto **ist gestohlen worden***. Her car **has been stolen**.

1 Choose the adjectives with the correct endings in these sentences.

a Das **kleine / kleines** Mädchen spielt mit der **große / großen** Puppe.

b Hast du mit dem **neue / neuen** Lehrer gesprochen?

c Man musste das **alte / alten** Dach der **kleine / kleinen** Kirche reparieren.

d Der **junge / jungen** Mann mit den **blaue / blauen** Haaren ist ihr Bruder.

e Die **ältere / älteren** Schwester ist nicht so intelligent wie die **jüngere / jüngeren**.

f Während der **lange / langen** Schulferien hat er die **schönste / schönsten** Strände besucht.

2 Add the correct adjectival endings in these sentences: look at articles and possessive adjectives to give you a clue about cases, number and gender.

a Sie wohnt in einem alt_____ Haus in der Nähe eines hübsch_____ Dorfes.

b Mein best_____ Freund hat vor kurzem ein gebraucht_____ Motorrad gekauft.

c In unserem groß_____ Garten befindet sich ein klein_____ Teich

mit einem schön_____ Brunnen.

d Bis jetzt haben wir leider keine gut_____ Freunde kennen gelernt.

e Wegen eines schwer___ Verkehrsunfalls mussten wir in einem

lang _____ Stau sitzen.

f Dort findet man keine modern_____ Hotels, nur eine toll_____ Aussicht auf das Meer.

g Während meiner lang_____ Schulferien habe ich meinen

deutsch _____ Austauschpartner besucht.

h Ein nett_____ Mädchen in meiner Klasse hat mir einen

interessant _____ Roman geschenkt.

Grammatik

An adjective following a noun does **not** need an ending:

Unser Haus ist ziemlich groß.

An adjective before a noun **always** needs an ending:

Wir haben ein ziemlich großes Haus.

There are three sets of endings, depending on what comes before the adjective. Choosing the correct ending depends on the case, number and gender of the noun.

Type 1

After the **definite article** (the word for 'the'), *dieser, jeder*, etc., add these endings:

	masc.	fem.	neuter	plural
nom.	-e	-e	-e	
acc.		-e	-e	
gen.				*-en*
dat.				

Der junge Mann wohnt in dem großen Haus.

Tipp

After *alles*, use the neuter endings, e.g. *alles Gute* – all the best.

Tipp

Learning complete tables can be difficult, so for Types 1 and 2, just memorise the endings in the L-shaped boxes. Every other ending in the tables is *-en*.

Type 2

After the **indefinite article** (the word for 'a'), *kein, mein*, etc., add the following endings:

	masc.	fem.	neuter	plural
nom.	-er	-e	-es	
acc.		-e	-es	
gen.				*-en*
dat.				

Ein neuer Computer wäre viel schneller.

Topic 4: Adjectival endings (continued)

3 Insert the correct adjectival endings in these sentences.

a Brasilianisch_____ Kaffee schmeckt lecker.

b Morgen gibt's schlecht_____ Wetter.

c Viele modern_____ Autos verbrauchen wenig Benzin.

d Sie trinkt gern französisch_____ Wein.

e Zum Frühstück isst er manchmal zwei gekocht_____ Eier.

f Magst du den Geruch von frisch gemäht_____ Gras?

g Er hat ein paar spanisch_____ Zeitschriften gelesen.

h In mehreren europäisch_____ Staaten ist die Arbeitslosigkeit ein Problem.

i Auf dem Markt müssen wir grün_____ Salat und frisch_____ Karotten kaufen.

j Innerhalb kurz_____ Zeit wurden einige indisch_____ Dörfer überflutet.

4 Translate these phrases into German.

a nothing cold _____

b something small _____

c little (that is) interesting _____

d much (that is) important _____

5 Add the correct adjectival endings (all types) in these sentences.

a Seine österreichisch_____Freundin hat ihm mehrere romantisch

_____ E-Mails geschrieben.

b Nach der lang_____ Reise wollte er eine groß_____ Tasse Tee.

c Mein jüngst_____ Bruder isst überhaupt kein roh_____ Gemüse.

d In der klein_____ Stadt gab es für ausländisch_____ Touristen nichts

Interessant_____.

e Die alt___ Dame hat sich leider den link_____ Arm gebrochen.

f Ich bin der fest_____ Meinung, dass wir sofort aus diesem schrecklich

_____Hotel ausziehen sollten.

g Sie würde alles Möglich_____ machen, um ihrer best_____ Freundin zu helfen.

h Im schön_____ Garten des alt_____ Hauses gab es ein paar japanisch_____

Bäume und viele exotisch_____ Blumen.

i Der reich_____ Vater meines amerikanisch___ Freundes hat sechs teur_____Autos.

j Diesen neu_____ Film dürfen unsere klein_____Kinder nicht sehen.

1 Starting with the underlined phrases or words, unscramble the rest of the sentence to make sense, using the future perfect tense. (Don't forget to use inversion.) Then translate the sentences into English.

a   aus dem Urlaub / werden / <u>Dieses Wochenende</u> / sein / meine Eltern / zurückgekommen.

_____

_____

b   haben / unseren neuen Kühlschrank / man / geliefert / <u>Bis morgen Nachmittag</u> / wird.

_____

_____

c   wir / <u>Durch dieses Training</u> / abgenommen / werden / in sechs Wochen / haben / fünf Kilo.

_____

_____

d   einen guten Job / haben / bekommen / ich / <u>Bis nächstes Jahr</u> / werde.

_____

_____

> ### Grammatik
> A compound tense is simply a combination of two tenses and has more than one word.
>
> The future perfect is used when talking about what <u>will have happened</u>. To form it, use the present tense of *werden* + past participle + *haben/sein*:
>
> *Bis nächste Woche **werde** ich meinen Aufsatz **geschrieben haben**.* By next week I **shall have written** my essay.
>
> Note that there is no difference between 'will' and 'shall' when translating into German.

2 Complete these sentences in the future perfect, inserting the correct part of *werden*, the past participle of the verb in brackets, and either *haben* or *sein*.

a   Morgen um diese Zeit _____ du hoffentlich deine Fahrprüfung _____

_____. **(bestehen)**

b   Mein Chef _____ meine E-Mail schon _____ _____ . **(bekommen)**

c   Nach 20 Jahren _____ sich viele Dinge _____ _____ . **(ändern)**

d   Innerhalb von sechs Jahren _____ ich vielleicht Pilot _____ _____ . **(werden)**

e   Die Lehrerin _____ wahrscheinlich nach Hause _____ _____ . **(gehen)**

f   _____ du bis Montag den Roman _____ _____ ? **(auslesen)**

3 Translate these phrases into German. Use the words in the box below to help you.

a   You (fam. sg.) will have already heard this song.

_____

b   By tomorrow he will have arrived in Tokyo.

_____

c   We will have made great progress.

_____

> die Lösung   schon   ankommen
> große Fortschritte   das Lied

d   By next year they will have found a solution.

_____

Topic 4: The conditional and conditional perfect

1 Complete the following sentence openings with the correct auxiliary verb.

a Wir würden mit dem Zug gefahren _____ , wenn ...

b Du würdest einen Preis gewonnen _____ , wenn ...

c Meine Schwester würde gestorben _____ , wenn ...

2 Alter these sentences to replace the conditional perfect with the imperfect subjunctive form. Then translate them into English.

a Seine Mutter würde ihn ins Krankenhaus gebracht haben.

_____

_____

b Wegen des Gewitters würde ich lieber zu Hause geblieben sein.

_____

_____

c Meine Verwandten würden gestern vorbeigekommen sein.

_____

_____

d Würdet ihr den Obdachlosen geholfen haben?

_____

_____

3 Translate these sentences into German, using first the conditional perfect and then the imperfect subjunctive. Use the words in the box alongside to help you.

Example: She would have seen me earlier. *Sie würde mich früher gesehen haben. Sie hätte mich früher gesehen*.

a They would have trained longer.

_____

b It would never have happened.

_____

c I would have sent them a text message.

_____

d My gran would have fallen down.

_____

Grammatik

The **conditional** (see page 45) is used to say what 'would happen':

*Ich **würde** meinen Freund **anrufen**.* I **would ring** my friend.

The **conditional perfect** (see page 41) is used to express the idea of 'would have happened':

*Ich **würde** meinen Freund **angerufen** haben* ... I **would have rung** my friend (if ...)

Tipp

When forming the conditional perfect, remember that the word 'have' is actually an auxiliary verb being used with the past participle. So think whether you will need *haben* or *sein*!

Grammatik

However, those conditional perfect forms, *würde ... haben* and *würde ... sein* can be replaced by *hätte* and *wäre*. These are **imperfect subjunctives** (see page 41). This shorter form is more commonly used in German.

*ich **hätte** ... (gemacht) = ich **würde** ... (gemacht) **haben** –* I would have done ...

*ich **wäre** ... (gefahren) = ich **würde** ... (gefahren) **sein** –* I would have gone ...

Compare this with the example above:

*Ich **hätte** meinen Freund **angerufen**,* ... I would have rung my friend (if, ...)

die SMS   hinfallen   länger
passieren   trainieren   nie

1 Identify whether these verbs are indicative (I) or subjunctive (S) or if they could be either (IS).

a du sagest ☐   **b** ich kaufe ☐   **c** sie geht ☐   **d** wir fahren ☐

e er trage ☐   **f** ihr habet ☐   **g** es gebe ☐   **h** sie lassen ☐

i er nehme ☐   **j** sie sieht ☐

2 Insert the correct form of Subjunctive 1 (present subjunctive) of the infinitive given in brackets.

a Mein Onkel sagte, er _____ sich nicht wohl. (**fühlen**)

b Unsere Lehrerin sagte, sie _____ in der Nähe der Schule. (**wohnen**)

c Die Kinder sagten, es _____ zu viele Leute auf dem Rummelplatz. (**geben**)

d Ihr Freund sagte, er _____ sie morgen um 11 Uhr. (**treffen**)

e Meine Cousine sagte, sie _____ nächstes Jahr. (**heiraten**)

f Der Lehrer sagte, er _____ das Fenster auf. (**machen**)

3 Complete the sentences with the correct form of the perfect subjunctive.

a Der Junge sagte, er _____ den Ball _____. (**verlieren**)

b Meine Mutter sagte uns, sie _____ einen Kuchen _____. (**backen**)

c Vati sagte, er _____ am Freitag nach Stuttgart _____. (**fahren**)

d Man sagte, sie _____ eine berühmte Schauspielerin _____. (**werden**)

e Der Direktor sagte, er _____ gerade mit meinen Eltern _____. (**sprechen**)

f Ihr Bruder sagte, er _____ erst um 13 Uhr _____. (**aufstehen**)

g Meine Schwester sagte, unsere Oma _____ im Sessel _____. (**einschlafen**)

h Der Mann sagte, er _____ seinen Hund nicht _____. (**finden**)

Grammatik

The **subjunctive** is used in indirect (reported) speech. There are two forms: **Subjunctive 1** and **Subjunctive 2**.

Note that the endings for regular and irregular verbs are exactly the same. Some endings are the same as for the present indicative (the form you already know). Here are the endings:

-e, *-est*, *-e*, *-en*, *-et*, *-en*

The only exception is *sein*:

ich sei
du seiest
er/sie/es sei
wir seien
ihr seiet
Sie/sie seien

Grammatik

When conveying indirect speech, English often changes the tense:

Direct speech – He said, "I am going to the cinema".

Indirect speech – He said he was going to the cinema.

However, German changes from the indicative to the subjunctive. Therefore, if what the speaker says is in the present tense in direct speech, use **Subjunctive 1** in indirect speech:

Direct speech – *Er sagte: „Ich gehe ins Kino."*

Indirect speech – *Er sagte, er gehe ins Kino.*

Sometimes the subjunctive form looks the same as the indicative. It will be explained later what to do in these cases.

If the speaker's words were in the past tense in direct speech, use **Subjunctive 1** with the past participle (perfect subjunctive):

Direct speech – *Er sagte: „Ich bin ins Kino gegangen."*

Indirect speech – *Er sagte, er sei ins Kino gegangen.*

Grammatik

If Subjunctive 1 looks the same as the present indicative, you must use **Subjunctive 2** (imperfect subjunctive) to show that what is being said is indirect speech.

Weak verbs in Subjunctive 2 are the same as the imperfect indicative (*machte, kaufte* etc.)

Strong verbs add the same ending to the imperfect stem as in Subjunctive 1, but if the vowel in the stem can add an umlaut, it does so.

	kommen	*wissen*	*gehen*	*schreiben*
ich	käme	wüsste	ginge	schriebe
du	kämest	wüsstest	gingest	schriebest
er/sie/es	käme	wüsste	ginge	schriebe
wir	kämen	wüssten	gingen	schrieben
ihr	kämet	wüsstet	ginget	schriebet
Sie/sie	kämen	wüssten	gingen	schrieben

1 Write down the Subjunctive 2 (imperfect subjunctive) form of these verbs.

a wir _____(schlafen)   f du _____(wissen)

b er_____(schicken)   g die Leute_____(werden)

c es_____(kommen)   h ihr _____(kaufen)

d Anton_____(gehen)   i ich_____(haben)

e ich_____(sein)   j Monika_____(geben)

2 Complete the sentences with the appropriate form of the subjunctive. (Use Subjunctive 1 wherever possible, provided that it is different from the indicative form – see Exercise 1 on page 59.)

Study this example: the Subjunctive 1 form would be *wissen* which is the same as the present indicative. Therefore, we must use the Subjunctive 2 form which is *wüssten*.

Example: Meine Eltern sagten, sie _____ es nicht. (**wissen**)

Meine Eltern sagten, sie *wüssten* es nicht.

a Die Dame sagte, der Zug _____ in zehn Minuten an. (**kommen**)

b Meine Freunde sagten, sie _____ morgen mit. (**kommen**)

c Er sagte, er _____ später eine E-Mail. (**schreiben**)

d Meine Schwestern sagten, sie _____ kein Geld. (**haben**)

e Mein Bruder sagte aber, er _____ viel Geld. (**haben**)

f Die Polizistin sagte, sie _____ so etwas noch nie _____. (**sehen**)

g Meine Brüder sagten, sie _____ ihre Hausaufgaben schon _____. (**machen**)

h Die Mutter meines Freundes sagte, er _____ sofort _____. (**ausgehen**)

Grammatik

You also use **Subjunctive 2** when talking about hypothetical situations, i.e. in **conditional sentences** (see page 45) and after *als ob* (as if):

*Er sah aus, **als ob** er krank **wäre**.* He looked as if he were ill.

*Sie tat, **als ob** sie müde **wäre**.* She pretended to be (acted as if she were) tired.

3 On a separate sheet of paper, translate these sentences into German. Use the words in the box to help you.

a They looked as if they were unhappy.   d She pretended to be in a hurry.

b He looked as if he hadn't eaten in days.   e The man acted as if nothing had happened.

c They looked as if they had no money.

seit Tagen
nichts
es
eilig haben
unglücklich
geschehen

1 Link the sentence halves so that they make sense. (More than one combination is sometimes possible.) Then translate the sentences into English underneath.

a	Es liegt an	1	Leben und Tod.
b	Es handelt sich um	2	einen Mordfall in der Karibik.
c	Es gilt,	3	keinen Grund dafür.
d	Es geht um	4	gut um sie.
e	Es gibt	5	seiner Hartnäckigkeit.
f	Es gefällt mir,	6	Mut zu zeigen.
g	Es heißt,	7	am Strand zu liegen.
h	Es steht	8	nichts.
i	Es fehlt mir an	9	die Zeit heilt alle Wunden.

_____

_____

_____

_____

_____

_____

_____

_____

2 Translate these sentences into German. Use the words in the box to help you.

a He likes going to the cinema.

_____

b I manage to prepare the evening meal.

_____

c It is necessary to save the euro.

_____

d We succeeded in finding a parking space.

_____

e She liked visiting her grandparents.

_____

f They managed to reach him.

_____

Grammatik

Many verbs can only be used in **impersonal** expressions, i.e. with *es*. When these expressions refer to a person, the dative case is normally used for the person. You already know how to use *es ist*, *es sind*, *es gibt* and *es* in weather expressions. Here are some other expressions:

Es fehlt mir an …	I lack …
Es gefällt mir, … zu tun	I like doing …
Es geht um …	It's about … / It's a matter of …
Es gilt, … zu tun	It is necessary to do …
Es handelt sich um …	It's about …
Es heißt, dass …	It is said that …
Es kommt auf etwas an.	It depends on sth.
Es liegt an …	It is due to …
Es steht schlecht um ihn.	Things look bad for him.

Tipp

Certain impersonal expressions are often used with an infinitive clause (see page 39), e.g.

Es gefällt mir, … zu tun. I like doing …
Es gilt, … zu tun. It is necessary to do …

Es gelingt mir, … zu tun. I manage to do …/I succeed in doing …

Example:
*Es ist ihm gelungen, die Reifenpanne **zu reparieren**.* He managed **to fix** the puncture.

der Euro   erreichen
der Parkplatz   retten
zubereiten

1 Write the infinitive for the verbs in the following sentences.

a Um wie viel Uhr fängt die Trauung an? _____

b Er hat seiner Oma das Simsen beigebracht. _____

c Abends ging er nie aus. _____

d Unsere Katze ist durch das Fenster gesprungen. _____

e Mein Freund lädt mich zu einer Party ein. _____

f Leider ist es mir nicht gelungen. _____

g Unser Opa ist nach dem Abendessen im Sessel eingeschlafen. _____

h Ihrer Meinung nach hat die Ehe mehr Sicherheit für die Kinder geboten. _____

2 Identify the different verb forms in the following sentences. Add a cross to the verbs in Subjunctive 1, underline the verbs in Subjunctive 2 and circle the verbs in the pluperfect.

a Meine Mutter hatte ihr Portemonnaie völlig vergessen.

b Er sagte, er sehe nicht gern fern.

c Nachdem unsere Verwandten abgefahren waren, gingen wir ins Bett.

d Wir würden ins Konzert gehen, wenn wir Karten hätten.

e Die Kinder sagten, sie seien sehr müde.

f Der Alte tat, als ob er krank wäre.

g Sie sagten, sie müssten später zurückkommen.

h Weil wir den letzten Bus verpasst hatten, mussten wir ein Taxi nehmen.

3 Rearrange the words into the correct order.

a gedacht – ich – nie – hätte – daran (*I would never have thought of that.*)

_____

b gesehen – habe – er – den Film – er – schon – sagte (*He said he had already seen the film.*)

_____

c mittlerweile – sein – angekommen – mein Verlobter – in Kanada – wird (*My fiancé will have arrived in Canada by now.*)

_____

d ohne – geht – machen – zum Zahnarzt – sie – zu – einen Termin (*She is going to the dentist's without making an appointment.*)

_____

e zu – hatte – eine Geschichte – er – um – trösten – seinen Sohn – erzählt – ihm (*In order to comfort his son, he had told him a story.*)

_____

f obdachlos – aus – die Alte – wäre – ob – sie – als – sah (*The old woman looked as if she were homeless.*)

_____

4a Read the text and underline the infinitives.

Die Ehe

A Die Hochzeit soll der schönste Tag im Leben sein. Ein Paar möchte für immer zusammenbleiben, und es bekennt dies öffentlich vor Familie und Freunden bei einem großen Fest und oft auch noch in der Kirche. Die Romantik dieses Moments ist immer noch ein beliebter Stoff für Kinofilme.

B Im vergangenen Jahr hat die Zahl der Eheschließungen um 14 Prozent abgenommen. Die Eltern meiner Freundin wollen zum Beispiel nur zusammenleben, denn Heiraten halten sie für unwichtig.

C Ich finde Heiraten toll, denn es verbindet zwei Menschen mehr als zuvor. Wenn man nicht verheiratet ist, fehlt etwas, finde ich. Ich bin für die Ehe und habe vor, eines Tages zu heiraten.

D Man kann nicht bei jeder Kleinigkeit einfach weglaufen, sondern muss sich Problemen stellen, Verantwortung tragen und Toleranz üben.

E Die große Mehrheit der Paare hat das Zusammenleben bereits in einer gemeinsamen Wohnung erprobt. Wahrscheinlich werden mein Freund und ich das genauso machen.

F Man sollte sich schon einige Zeit kennen lernen, um herauszufinden, ob das Gegenüber auch wirklich „der/die Richtige" ist.

G Es gibt steuerliche Vorteile, wenn man verheiratet ist.

4b Which of the infinitives you have underlined are separable verbs? Write them down.

_____

4c Select the title from the box below that matches to each paragraph. Note down the correct letter.

Titel	Absatz
1 Die meisten Ehepaare haben schon vor der Ehe zusammengelebt.	
2 Es gibt finanzielle Gründe, warum man heiraten sollte.	
3 Immer weniger Leute wollen heiraten.	
4 Man sollte warten, bevor man heiratet.	
5 Wenn man sich liebt, dann soll man heiraten.	
6 Für das Ehepaar ist heute ohne Zweifel der wichtigste Tag.	
7 In jeder Ehe gibt es Schwierigkeiten.	

1a Lesen Sie die folgenden Äußerungen über den besten Vater und ergänzen Sie die fehlenden Adjektivendungen.

Wer ist der beste Vater?

Leo

Ein gut___ Vater widmet sich täglich mindestens eine bis zwei Stunden seinen klein___ Kindern. Am Wochenende sind es täglich drei bis vier Stunden. In dieser Zeit kümmert sich dieser ideal___ Vater ausschließlich und intensiv um die Kinder.

Marion

Der gut___ Papa spielt viel mit seinen Kindern, tobt mit ihnen herum und ist zum Kuscheln da. Sport und Toben fördern die motorisch___ Fähigkeiten. Er erklärt ihnen die Welt oder erforscht gemeinsam mit den Kindern neu___ Wissensgebiete.

Richard

Der Vater beteiligt sich auch an den wichtig___ Erziehungsaufgaben und sorgt für eine konsequent___ Umsetzung der festgesetzt___ Regeln. Der ideal___ Vater wäscht, spült und säubert genauso viel wie seine Partnerin.

Sara

Natürlich trägt der perfekt___ Vater mit einem Job zur finanziell___ Sicherheit der Familie bei. Er ist aber nicht unbedingt alleinig___ Versorger, weil idealerweise die Mutter sich auch beruflich verwirklichen kann. Leider wurde der ideal___ Vater noch nirgends gesehen. Es ist ja für eine Person auch fast unmöglich, so viele groß___ Anforderungen zu erfüllen.

1b Lesen Sie die Texte noch einmal. Schreiben Sie dann den passenden Namen (Leo, Marion, Richard, Sara) zu jeder Aussage.

a Es ist besser, wenn beide Elternteile Geld verdienen können. _____

b Mit einem guten Vater im Haus gibt es keine traditionelle Arbeitsverteilung. _____

c Ein Vater sollte viel Zeit mit seinem Kind verbringen. _____

d Der beste Vater existiert nicht. _____

e Disziplin ist in jeder Familie wichtig. _____

f Der Vater muss in vielfacher Weise die Entwicklung des Kindes unterstützen. _____

2 Ergänzen Sie die folgenden zehn Sätze mit der richtigen Form der Adjektive oder Verben.

a   Leider hat er keine _____ Freunde in seiner Klasse. (**richtig**)

b   Ein _____ Vater hat das Geld für seine Familie verdient. (**traditionell**)

c   Man darf dieses _____ Problem nicht ignorieren. (**klein**)

d   Sie kennt Leute aus vielen _____ Ländern. (**asiatisch**)

e   Wir trafen unsere Freunde, nachdem wir zu Abend gegessen _____. (**haben**)

f   Wenn ich das gewusst hätte, _____ ich nicht nach Köln gefahren. (**sein**)

g   Mein Freund Jakob hat mich nie im Stich _____. (**lassen**)

h   Es wäre ideal, wenn du mich um zehn Uhr treffen _____. (**können**)

i   Daniel und seine Freundin haben ihre Probleme gemeinsam _____. (**lösen**)

j   Die Zahl der Scheidungen ist letztes Jahr leicht _____. (**steigen**)

3 Ergänzen Sie die folgenden zehn Sätze mit der richtigen Form der Adjektive oder Verben.

a   Wegen des _____ Wetters konnte die Hochzeit nicht im Freien stattfinden. (**schlecht**)

b   In der _____ Gesellschaft hat sich die Rolle der Großeltern gewandelt. (**heutig**)

c   Ich habe einige _____ Freunde in der Schweiz. (**gut**)

d   Die Erlebnisse _____ Väter sind heutzutage etwas anders als früher. (**neu**)

e   Meine Freundin und ich haben ein paar Probleme in unserer Beziehung _____. (**erkennen**)

f   Karlas Mutter sagte, sie _____ mit ihr nicht mehr reden. (**wollen**)

g   Wenn mein Vater das gewusst hätte, _____ er bestimmt sauer gewesen. (**sein**)

h   Als wir letztes Jahr meine Tante besuchten, _____ sie schon zehn Kilo abgenommen. (**haben**)

i   Ich _____ dich anrufen, wenn der Zug Verspätung hätte. (**müssen**)

j   Sonja starrte ihn an, als ob sie ein Gespenst gesehen _____. (**haben**)

The more common irregular verbs

The forms of compound verbs are the same as for the basic verbs, e.g. *anfangen* has the same irregularities as fangen. * Verbs which take *sein* in the perfect tense.

infinitive	3rd person sing. present	imperfect indicative	past participle	English
backen	bäckt	backte/buk (old)	gebacken	to bake
befehlen	befiehlt	befahl	befohlen	to order
beginnen	beginnt	begann	begonnen	to begin
beißen	beißt	biss	gebissen	to bite
bewegen	bewegt	bewog	bewogen	to move
biegen	biegt	bog	gebogen	to bend
bieten	bietet	bot	geboten	to offer
binden	bindet	band	gebunden	to tie
bitten	bittet	bat	gebeten	to ask
blasen	bläst	blies	geblasen	to blow
bleiben	bleibt	blieb	geblieben*	to stay
braten	brät	briet	gebraten	to roast, fry
brechen	bricht	brach	gebrochen	to break
brennen	brennt	brannte	gebrannt	to burn
bringen	bringt	brachte	gebracht	to bring
denken	denkt	dachte	gedacht	to think
dringen	dringt	drang	gedrungen*	to penetrate, push
dürfen	darf	durfte	gedurft	to be allowed to
empfangen	empfängt	empfing	empfangen	to receive
empfehlen	empfiehlt	empfahl	empfohlen	to recommend
empfinden	empfindet	empfand	empfunden	to feel
erschrecken	erschrickt	erschrak / erschreckte	erschrocken	to scare
essen	isst	aß	gegessen	to eat
fahren	fährt	fuhr	gefahren*	to go, travel, drive
fallen	fällt	fiel	gefallen*	to fall
fangen	fängt	fing	gefangen	to catch
finden	findet	fand	gefunden	to find
fliegen	fliegt	flog	geflogen*	to fly
fliehen	flieht	floh	geflohen*	to flee
fließen	fließt	floss	geflossen*	to flow
fressen	frisst	fraß	gefressen	to eat (of animals)
frieren	friert	fror	gefroren	to freeze
geben	gibt	gab	gegeben	to give
gehen	geht	ging	gegangen*	to go
gelingen	gelingt	gelang	gelungen*	to succeed
gelten	gilt	galt	gegolten	to be valid, count
genießen	genießt	genoss	genossen	to enjoy
geschehen	geschieht	geschah	geschehen*	to happen
gewinnen	gewinnt	gewann	gewonnen	to win
gießen	gießt	goss	gegossen	to pour
gleichen	gleicht	glich	geglichen	to resemble
gleiten	gleitet	glitt	geglitten*	to slide

AQA German AS © Oxford University Press. Photocopying prohibited

infinitive	3rd person sing. present	imperfect indicative	past participle	English
graben	gräbt	grub	gegraben	to dig
greifen	greift	griff	gegriffen	to grasp
haben	hat	hatte	gehabt	to have
halten	hält	hielt	gehalten	to stop
hängen	hängt	hing	gehangen	to hang
heben	hebt	hob	gehoben	to lift
heißen	heißt	hieß	geheißen	to be called
helfen	hilft	half	geholfen	to help
kennen	kennt	kannte	gekannt	to know
klingen	klingt	klang	geklungen	to sound
kommen	kommt	kam	gekommen*	to come
können	kann	konnte	gekonnt	to be able to
kriechen	kriecht	kroch	gekrochen	to creep
laden	lädt	lud	geladen	to load
lassen	lässt	ließ	gelassen	to allow
laufen	läuft	lief	gelaufen*	to run
leiden	leidet	litt	gelitten	to suffer
leihen	leiht	lieh	geliehen	to lend
lesen	liest	las	gelesen	to read
liegen	liegt	lag	gelegen	to lie
lügen	lügt	log	gelogen	to tell a lie
meiden	meidet	mied	gemieden	to avoid
messen	misst	maß	gemessen	to measure
mögen	mag	mochte	gemocht	to like
müssen	muss	musste	gemusst	to have to
nehmen	nimmt	nahm	genommen	to take
nennen	nennt	nannte	genannt	to name
pfeifen	pfeift	pfiff	gepfiffen	to whistle
raten	rät	riet	geraten	to guess
reiben	reibt	rieb	gerieben	to rub
reiten	reitet	ritt	geritten	to ride
reißen	reißt	riss	gerissen	to rip
reiten	reitet	ritt	geritten*	to ride
rennen	rennt	rannte	gerannt*	to run
riechen	riecht	roch	gerochen	to smell
rufen	ruft	rief	gerufen	to call
saugen	saugt	saugte / sog	gesaugt / gesogen	to suck
schaffen	schafft	schuf	geschaffen	to manage
scheiden	scheidet	schied	geschieden*	to separate
scheinen	scheint	schien	geschienen	to shine
schieben	schiebt	schob	geschoben	to push, shove
schießen	schießt	schoss	geschossen	to shoot
schlafen	schläft	schlief	geschlafen	to sleep
schlagen	schlägt	schlug	geschlagen	to hit
schleichen	schleicht	schlich	geschlichen*	to creep, sneak
schließen	schließt	schloss	geschlossen	to shut

infinitive	3rd person sing. present	imperfect indicative	past participle	English
schmelzen	schmilzt	schmolz	geschmolzen	to melt
schneiden	schneidet	schnitt	geschnitten	to cut
schreiben	schreibt	schrieb	geschrieben	to write
schreien	schreit	schrie	geschrie(e)n	to cry
schwimmen	schwimmt	schwamm	geschwommen*	to swim
schweigen	schweigt	schwieg	geschwiegen	to be silent
schwören	schwört	schwor	geschworen	to swear
sehen	sieht	sah	gesehen	to see
sein	ist	war	gewesen*	to be
senden	sendet	sandte	gesandt	to send
singen	singt	sang	gesungen	to sing
sinken	sinkt	sank	gesunken*	to sink
sitzen	sitzt	saß	gesessen	to sit
sollen	soll	sollte	gesollt	to be supposed to
sprechen	spricht	sprach	gesprochen	to speak
springen	springt	sprang	gesprungen*	to jump
stehen	steht	stand	gestanden*	to stand
stehlen	stiehlt	stahl	gestohlen	to steal
steigen	steigt	stieg	gestiegen*	to climb
sterben	stirbt	starb	gestorben*	to die
stoßen	stößt	stieß	gestoßen	to push
streichen	streicht	strich	gestrichen	to paint, stroke
streiten	streitet	stritt	gestritten	to quarrel, argue
tragen	trägt	trug	getragen	to carry
treffen	trifft	traf	getroffen	to meet
treiben	treibt	trieb	getrieben	to do
treten	tritt	trat	getreten	to step
trinken	trinkt	trank	getrunken	to drink
tun	tut	tat	getan	to do
verderben	verdirbt	verdarb	verdorben	to spoil
vergessen	vergisst	vergaß	vergessen	to forget
verlieren	verliert	verlor	verloren	to lose
verschwinden	verschwindet	verschwand	verschwunden*	to disappear
verzeihen	verzeiht	verzieh	verziehen	to pardon
wachsen	wächst	wuchs	gewachsen*	to grow
waschen	wäscht	wusch	gewaschen	to wash
weisen	weist	wies	gewiesen	to show, point out
wenden	wendet	wandte	gewendet	to turn
werben	wirbt	warb	geworben	to advertise
werden	wird	wurde	geworden*	to become
werfen	wirft	warf	geworfen	to throw
wiegen	wiegt	wog	gewogen	to weigh
wissen	weiß	wusste	gewusst	to know
wollen	will	wollte	gewollt	to want to
ziehen	zieht	zog	gezogen	to pull
zwingen	zwingt	zwang	gezwungen	to compel

The present tense

Formation of regular verbs

To form the present tense of regular (weak) verbs, take off the final -en or -n from the infinitive and add back the endings as shown in the two examples below:

spielen	to play	lernen	to learn
ich spiele		ich lerne	
du spielst		du lernst	
er/sie/es spielt		er/sie/es lernt	
ihr spielt		ihr lernt	
wir spielen		wir lernen	
Sie/sie spielen		Sie/sie lernen	

For verbs whose stem ends in 'd' or 't', or in 'n' or 'm' after a consonant, the letter 'e' must be added before the present tense verb ending, e.g.

landen – to land	warten – to wait	öffnen – to open	widmen – to dedicate
ich lande	ich warte	ich öffne	ich widme
du landest	du wartest	du öffnest	du widmest
er/sie/es landet	er/sie/es wartet	er/sie/es öffnet	er/sie /es widmet
wir landen	wir warten	wir öffnen	wir widmen
etc.	etc.	etc.	etc.

Formation of irregular verbs

Some verbs are irregular in the present tense. Three very important irregular verbs are:

haben to have	sein to be	werden to become
ich bin	ich lerne	ich werde
du bist	du lernst	du wirst
er/sie/es ist	er/sie/es lernt	er/sie/es wird
wir sind	ihr lernt	wir werden
ihr seid	wir lernen	ihr werdet
Sie/sie sind	Sie/sie lernen	Sie/sie werden

Irregular verbs do not have quite the same pattern as regular verbs. However, the differences are only slight and are to be found in the *du, er, sie* and *es* forms of the verb. Sometimes you add an *umlaut* (ö, ä, ü) and sometimes there is a vowel change:

	fahren to drive	laufen to run	tragen to carry
du	fährst	läufst	trägst
er/sie/es	fährt	läuft	trägt

Other useful verbs which change in the same way are:

empfangen	to receive
fallen	to fall
fangen	to catch
halten	to stop
schlafen	to sleep
schlagen	to hit
tragen	to carry/wear
waschen	to wash

Some common irregular verbs where there is a vowel change are:

	du	er/sie/es
essen	isst	isst
helfen	hilfst	hilft
lesen	liest	liest
nehmen	nimmst	nimmt
sehen	siehst	sieht
sprechen	sprichst	spricht
treffen	triffst	trifft
vergessen	vergisst	vergisst
wissen	weißt	weiß

The imperfect tense/simple past tense

The imperfect tense is also called the simple past tense, because the verb consists of just one element. The imperfect can be used for any action in the past and has the same meaning as the perfect tense (*ich spielte* = I played, I used to play, I was playing, I did play).

Weak (regular) verbs add the endings shown below to the stem of the verb.

ich	spiel**te**
du	spiel**test**
er/sie/es	spiel**te**
ihr	spiel**tet**
wir	spiel**ten**
Sie	spiel**ten**
sie	spiel**ten**

Strong (irregular) verbs change their stem in the imperfect and each form has to be learnt.

Remember that the *ich* form of the imperfect of irregular verbs is the same as the *er, sie* and *es* forms. Add -*st* to the *du* form and -*t* to the *ihr* form. For *wir, Sie* and *sie*, simply add -*en* to the stem.

ich	ging
du	ging**st**
er/sie/es	ging
ihr	ging**t**
wir	ging**en**
Sie	ging**en**
sie	ging**en**

Mixed verbs combine a change in their stem with -*te* endings of the regular verbs.

haben – ich hatte
kennen – ich kannte
wissen – ich wusste
bringen – ich brachte
verbringen – ich verbrachte
denken – ich dachte
rennen – ich rannte
nennen – ich nannte
brennen – ich brannte

Watch out for *sein* (to be):

ich	war
du	warst
er/sie/es	war
wir	waren
ihr	wart
Sie/sie	waren

The most irregular verb is *werden* (to become). It ends in -*de* instead of -*te*:

ich	wurde
du	wurdest
er/sie/es	wurde
wir	wurden
ihr	wurdet
Sie/sie	wurden

Modal verbs in the past tense are mostly used in their imperfect form:

	können	*dürfen*	*müssen*	*wollen*	*sollen*	*mögen*
ich	konnte	durfte	musste	wollte	sollte	mochte
du	konntest	durftest	musstest	wolltest	solltest	mochtest
er/sie/es	konnte	durfte	musste	wollte	sollte	mochte
wir	konnten	durften	mussten	wollten	sollten	mochten
ihr	konntet	durftet	musstet	wolltet	solltet	mochtet
Sie/sie	konnten	durften	mussten	wollten	sollten	mochten

ransition **from GCSE**
ersonal pronouns (page 5)

Er, **b** Sie, **c** Sie, **d** Es, **e** Sie, **f** Er, **g** sie

Sie hat mir einen Bleistift geliehen.
Hast du ihr die Karte geschickt?
Er hat es ihnen gegeben.
Habt ihr es uns nicht gebracht?
Sie hat ihm ein Foto versprochen.

She lent me a pencil.
Have you sent her the card?
He gave it to them.
Haven't you brought us it?
She promised him a photo.

Sie, ihnen, **b** Sie, ihn, **c** Er, es, **d** Wir, ihm, **e** Sie, dich, **f** Ihr, es, ihm,
ch, Ihnen, **h** Er, mir

e present tense (page 6)

r kaufst – kauft, **b** Sie lernen →, **c** ich kochst – koche, **d** wir
ielen →, **e** sie wohnt →, **f** ich machen – mache,
du glaube – glaubst, **h** wir trennen →, **i** ihr sucht →

sucht, **b** wohnen, **c** kaufe, **d** wartet, **e** lernen, **f** machst, **g** trennt,
endet

u	t	h	c	i	r	p	s	l
t	b	t	n	s	k	c	l	i
w	r	b	i	z	h	g	r	e
ä	i	h	s	l	q	i	n	s
s	t	g	ä	r	t	b	u	t
c	s	f	n	f	g	s	v	q
h	s	i	e	h	s	t	v	z
t	f	l	i	h	z	k	g	s

r spricht, **b** wir lesen, **c** du hilfst, **d** ich sehe, **e** sie gibt,
r empfehlt, **g** sie stiehlt, **h** sie schlafen

e perfect tense (page 7)

abe, **b** hat, **c** ist, **d** haben, **e** habt, **f** bin, **g** ist, **h** hat, **i** Hast, **j** sind

gemacht – We took/have taken photos of the wedding.
gebrochen – The boy broke/has broken his arm.
gefunden – I found this TV programme boring.
gefahren – We went/travelled into the town centre yesterday.
geholfen – She helped/has helped her/their sister with her
homework.

ch habe den Film gesehen.
Er hat meine E-Mail erhalten.
Wir sind in diesem Hotel geblieben.
Meine Mutter ist einkaufen gegangen.
Hast du das Geld gefunden?
Die Kinder haben im Park Fußball gespielt.

The imperfect tense (page 8)

1
a war, hatte, **b** waren, **c** waren, hatten, **d** warst, **e** hatte, **f** war, hatte

2
a wollten, **b** musste, **c** sollte, **d** durften, **e** konnten

3
a wollte, **b** konnte, **c** mussten, **d** durften, **e** sollte, **f** musste,
g Durfte, **h** konnte

Nominative and accusative cases (page 9)

1
a Das Mädchen hat heute den Schlüssel verloren.
b Der Lehrer hat einen Volkswagen.
c Am Wochenende muss der Mann den Rasen mähen.
d In der Pause essen meine Freunde und ich einen Schokoriegel
oder eine Banane.
e Mit ihrem Sohn hat sie überhaupt keine Geduld.
f Die Schülerin hat keinen Kuli und kein Heft.
g Den Hund habe ich nicht gesehen.
h Gestern hat ein Junge einen Zwanzigeuroschein im Park
gefunden.
i Der Mann und die Frau haben das Haus gekauft.
j Die Dame kennt der Mann nicht.

2
a Der Junge hat ein Portemonnaie gefunden.
b Ich habe ein Meerschweinchen und eine Katze, aber keinen
Goldfisch.
c Am Donnerstag besichtigen wir den Fernsehturm.
d Die Kinder haben den Film schon gesehen.
e In der Zukunft möchte ich ein Haus auf dem Land.
f Das Mädchen hat mir eine Geburtstagskarte geschickt.
g Gestern hat sie keine E-Mails bekommen.
h Den Mann kenne ich gar nicht.

Genitive and dative cases (page 10)

1
a Die Lehrerin hat dem Kind einen Kuli gegeben.
b Er wollte den Obdachlosen kein Geld geben.
c Die Kundin hat dem Hotelleiter einen Brief geschrieben.
d Ich habe einer Freundin eine E-Mail geschickt.

2
a Ich habe der Lehrerin die Fotos gezeigt.
I showed the teacher the photos./I showed the photos to the
teacher.
b Der Mann im Verkehrsamt hat der Familie ein preiswertes Hotel
empfohlen.
The man in the tourist information office recommended a
reasonable hotel to the family.
c Mein Bruder hat einem Freund einen alten Tennisschläger
geliehen.
My brother (has) lent a friend an old tennis racquet./My brother
(has) lent an old tennis racquet to a friend.
d Dem Chef habe ich kein Wort gesagt.
I didn't say/haven't said a word to the boss.
e Die Ärztin hat einem Mann die Tabletten verschrieben.
The doctor (has) prescribed a man the tablets./The doctor (has)
prescribed the tablets for a man.

3
a Unsere Lehrerin hat der Klasse eine Geschichte vorgelesen.
Our teacher read a story to the class.
b Die Eltern geben den Mädchen kein Taschengeld.
The parents don't give the girls any pocket money.
c Die Schülerin hat einer Freundin eine Zigarette angeboten.
The schoolgirl offered a cigarette to a friend.
d Jürgen hat der Firma den Lebenslauf geschickt.
Jürgen has sent the firm the CV.

Dative trigger verbs (page 11)

1

a3 Nach dem Fußballspiel hat der Manager der Mannschaft gratuliert.

b1 Die Fischgerichte auf der Speisekarte haben den Kindern nicht geschmeckt.

c2 Das Handy hat dem Jungen nicht gehört.

d5 Die Lehrerin versucht, es den Schülerinnen zu erklären.

e6 Da ich den Mann nicht gekannt habe, habe ich ihm nicht vertraut.

f4 Leider konnte der Arzt den Leuten nicht helfen.

Word order with two objects (page 11)

2

a Mein Bruder hat dem Verkäufer das Geld gegeben.

b Ein Lehrer hat es dem Schüler erklärt.

c Der Mann bringt der Frau einen Blumenstrauß.

d Meine Schwester hat mir den iPod geliehen.

e Ich habe einem Freund den tollen Roman empfohlen.

Word order: inversion, time–manner–place (page 12)

1

a Jeden Tag fährt meine Mutter zur Arbeit.

b In unserer Stadt gibt es keine Bibliothek.

c Zwei- oder dreimal pro Woche gehe ich joggen.

d Gestern mussten wir unsere Katze zum Tierarzt bringen.

e Nach zwei Wochen auf Zypern war ich völlig entspannt.

f Ab und zu gehen meine Familie und ich ins Restaurant.

2

There is more than one correct version possible. These are examples:

a Ich fahre nächstes Jahr ohne meine Familie nach Mallorca.

b Wir gehen manchmal zu Fuß in die Stadt.

c Er ist zum ersten Mal allein ins Ausland gefahren.

d Ich war eine Woche lang mit Freunden auf einem Campingplatz.

3

Suggested answers:

a Nächstes Jahr fahre ich ohne meine Familie nach Mallorca.

b Manchmal gehen wir zu Fuß in die Stadt.

c Zum ersten Mal ist er allein ins Ausland gefahren.

d Eine Woche lang war ich mit Freunden auf einem Campingplatz.

Word order: conjunctions (page 13)

1

a oder, **b** denn, **c** und, **d** denn, **e** sondern/denn

2

a Im Moment darf ich nicht fliegen, weil ich Probleme mit meinen Ohren habe.

b In der Zukunft wird sie in Deutschland arbeiten, da sie ihre Sprachkenntnisse verbessern möchte.

c Mein Bruder fährt sehr gern Rad, wenn er Zeit hat.

d Sie wird einen Job suchen, nachdem sie die Schule verlassen hat.

e Ich muss meiner Mutter beim Abwaschen helfen, bevor ich ausgehen darf.

f Mein Bruder hat viele Freunde kennen gelernt, während er in Frankreich gewohnt hat.

g Sie weiß noch nicht, ob sie morgen auf die Party gehen darf.

h Wir fahren immer mit der U-Bahn, wenn wir ins Stadtzentrum fahren wollen.

3

a Weil ich Probleme mit meinen Ohren habe, darf ich im Moment nicht fliegen.

b Da sie ihre Sprachkenntnisse verbessern möchte, wird sie in der Zukunft in Deutschland arbeiten.

c Wenn er Zeit hat, fährt mein Bruder sehr gern Rad.

d Nachdem sie die Schule verlassen hat, wird sie einen Job suchen.

e Bevor ich ausgehen darf, muss ich meiner Mutter beim Abwaschen helfen.

f Während er in Frankreich gewohnt hat, hat mein Bruder viele Freunde kennen gelernt.

g Ob sie morgen auf die Party gehen darf, weiß sie noch nicht.

h Wenn wir ins Stadtzentrum fahren wollen, fahren wir immer mit der U-Bahn.

Topic 1
The present tense (page 14)

1

a findet, **b** regnet, **c** arbeitest, **d** bedeutet

2

a Ich hole meine Oma am Flughafen ab.

b Weil die Sendung doof ist, schaltet er den Fernseher aus.

c Nächstes Jahr nimmt mein Cousin am Schüleraustausch teil.

d Jeden Morgen wachen die Kinder so früh auf.

e Der Reisebus fährt immer pünktlich ab.

f Abends sieht der Junge stundenlang fern.

3

separable	inseparable
einladen	besitzen
auskommen	verlangen
weggehen	gefallen
beitragen	entkommen
anbieten	widersprechen
zuhören	misslingen
stattfinden	empfinden
einführen	zerreißen
abfliegen	erwähnen
umsteigen	
aufmachen	

4

a Ich fahre jeden Morgen um 8 Uhr ab.

b Sie besucht ihren Mann im Krankenhaus.

c Meine Freunde kommen bald an.

d Ich verspreche ihm das Geld.

Gender of nouns (page 15)

1

German noun	English
a das Datum	date
b die Hoffnung	hope
c das Hindernis	obstacle
d der Löffel	spoon
e die Enkelin	granddaughter
f der Tourismus	tourism
g die Organisation	organisation
h der Passant	passer-by
i die Dunkelheit	darkness
j die Erlaubnis	permission
k der Frühling	spring
l das Häuschen	cottage
m der Rassismus	racism
n die Tastatur	keyboard
o die Allianz	alliance

2

German noun	English
a der Geld<u>beutel</u>	purse
b das Satelliten<u>fernsehen</u>	satellite TV
c die Kontakt<u>börse</u>	dating agency
d der Straßen<u>musikant</u>	street musician
e die Verbraucher<u>zufriedenheit</u>	consumer satisfaction
f das Koffer<u>radio</u>	portable radio
g die Autobahnrast<u>stätte</u>	motorway services
h das Betriebs<u>praktikum</u>	work experience
i der Fernseh<u>sender</u>	TV station
j die Werbe<u>aktion</u>	advertising campaign

Qualifiers (page 16)

More than one correct answer is possible. These are examples:
Der Dokumentarkanal hat mir <u>besonders</u> gefallen.
I particularly liked the documentary channel.
Es war <u>fast</u> unmöglich, den Film zu verstehen.
It was almost impossible to understand the film.
Vor kurzem habe ich ein <u>wirklich</u> interessantes Buch gelesen.
Recently, I read a really interesting book.
In unserer kleinen Stadt gibt es <u>kaum</u> Geschäfte.
In our small town there are hardly any shops.
Weil die Straße so nass war, ist sie <u>sehr</u> vorsichtig gefahren.
Because the road was so wet, she drove very carefully.
Das Hotel war luxuriös, aber <u>recht</u> teuer.
The hotel was luxurious but quite expensive.

Students' own answers.

The perfect tense (page 16)

a rasiert, **b** ausgeschaltet, **c** gelandet, **d** verkauft, **e** geöffnet,
f ausgekommen, **g** erlebt, **h** abgetrocknet

The perfect tense (page 17)

1

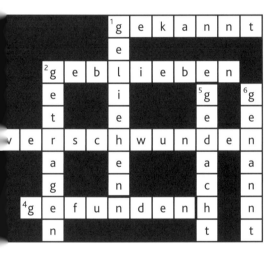

a gegeben, **b** verloren, **c** geschienen, **d** geschlafen, **e** gesehen,
f getrieben, **g** gestiegen, **h** gebrannt

2

a Letzte Woche habe ich meinen Onkel angerufen.
b Mein Freund hat einen Fehler entdeckt.
c Sie hat heute keine E-Mails geschickt/gesandt.
d Wir haben den Artikel in der Zeitung gelesen.
e Meine Tante hat mir ein Geschenk gebracht.
f Er ist am Wochenende abgefahren.
g Hat der Film schon angefangen/begonnen?
h Wir haben die Lehrerin nicht verstanden.

Indefinite pronouns (page 18)

a jemanden, **b** Niemand, **c** niemanden, **d** jemand, **e** jemandem,
f Niemand, **g** niemandem, **h** jemand, **i** niemandem, **j** Jemand

Interrogative adjectives (page 19)

1
a welchem, **b** Welche, **c** Welche, **d** welchem, **e** Welches, **f** Welcher,
g welchem, **h** Welcher

2
a Jenes, **b** Dieser, **c** jeder, **d** diesem, **e** jede, **f** dieser, **g** Jedes,
h Dieser, jener

The passive: present and imperfect tenses (page 20)

1
a A, **b** P, **c** P, **d** P, **e** A, **f** P

2
a Sein Handy <u>wurde</u> im Park <u>gefunden</u>.
b Die neuen Lautsprecher <u>werden</u> heute <u>geliefert</u>.
c Unser Sportzentrum <u>wurde</u> vom Bürgermeister <u>eröffnet</u>.
d Wir <u>wurden</u> durch den Verkehr <u>aufgehalten</u>.
e Die Zeitschrift <u>wird</u> von meiner Mutter <u>gelesen</u>.
f Das Internet <u>wurde</u> zunächst als militärisches Netz <u>entwickelt</u>.
g Weil es viel schneit, <u>werden</u> die Kinder früh nach Hause <u>geschickt</u>.
h Eine neue Schule <u>wird</u> dieses Jahr <u>gebaut</u>.

3
a Unsere Schule wurde im 19. Jahrhundert gegründet.
b Der Fernseher wurde gestern gestohlen.
c Das Auto wird von meiner Schwester gekauft.
d Zwei Frauen wurden bei dem Unfall verletzt.

The passive: other tenses (page 21)

1
a A man was/has been knocked down by a car.
b An eagle had been sighted in the park yesterday.
c The emails were/have been deleted.
d New measures had been introduced.
e Our car was/has been repaired today.
f These letters were/have been written by my sister.
g At the start of the 20th century the internet had not been invented.
h Has the thief not been caught yet?

2
a Die Miete muss einen Monat im Voraus bezahlt werden.
The rent has to be paid one month in advance.
b Diese Tatsache darf nicht vergessen werden.
This fact must not be forgotten.
c Die Äpfel mussten leider weggeworfen werden.
The apples had to be thrown away, unfortunately.
d Dieses Formular muss zuerst ausgefüllt werden.
This form must be filled in first.
e Alle Kinder sollten gegen Masern geimpft werden.
All children should be vaccinated against measles.

Prepositions and cases (page 22)

1
a durch, **b** bis, **c** ohne, **d** für
2
a gegenüber, **b** seit, **c** von, **d** nach
3
a ein, **b** den, **c** die, **d** dem (im), **e** das (ans), **f** dem (im)
4
a des Wetter<u>s</u>, **b** der Herbstferien, **c** einer Woche, **d** eines Unfall<u>s</u>,
e der Kinder, **f** der Geschäftszeiten

The future tense (page 23)

1
a Das Konzert wird um 19.30 Uhr beginnen./Um 19.30 Uhr wird das Konzert beginnen.
b Ich werde im August nach Schottland fahren./Im August werde ich nach Schottland fahren.
c Wir werden zehn Tage in Italien bleiben./Zehn Tage werden wir in Italien bleiben.
d Meine Eltern werden am Sonntag nach Hause zurückkommen./Am Sonntag werden meine Eltern nach Hause zurückkommen.
e Die Überfahrt wird etwa anderthalb Stunden dauern./Etwa anderthalb Stunden wird die Überfahrt dauern.
f Die Post wird gegen elf Uhr kommen./Gegen elf Uhr wird die Post kommen.

2

a The TV will be repaired on Tuesday.

b The photos will be uploaded soon.

c A letter will be sent by the headteacher.

d My children will be collected/picked up by their aunt after the film.

e A few days before the open-air concert, the stage will be set up.

f Hopefully/It is hoped that the fire will soon be extinguished.

g Fortunately, the old, empty buildings in the town centre will soon be demolished.

h Our new kitchen will be fitted tomorrow.

Mixed practice (page 24)

1

a Handys sind in unserer Schule verboten worden.

b Die Probleme mit dem Internet können nicht sofort gelöst werden.

c Bessere Elektroautos werden heutzutage entwickelt.

d Immer mehr Zeit wird vor dem Fernseher verschwendet.

e Das Handy wurde in den USA erfunden.

f Werbung wird überall im Internet angeschaut.

g Viele Kunden waren von der Werbung manipuliert worden.

h Leider werden Handys oft missbraucht.

2

a das, b der, c den, d diesem, keine, e der, f eine, einer, g Der, ein, dem, h die, der, i einem, die

3

Students' own answers.

Test yourself (page 25)

1

e, c, b, a, d

2

a kann, b gekostet, c fernsieht, d wird, e informiert, f vergessen, g beschwert, h wächst, i darf, j erhalten

Topic 2
The perfect tense (page 26)

1

weak	strong	mixed
gespielt	ausgezogen	gerannt
ausgeschaltet	erhalten	gebrannt
geendet	getragen	
verpasst	gerufen	
gesetzt	begonnen	
beeilt	gelesen	
ersetzt	gefroren	
	entschieden	

2

Students' own answers.

The imperfect tense: weak verbs (page 27)

1

a erzählte, b kauften, c landeten, d besuchte, e antwortetest, f dauerte, endete, g zeigte, h amüsierten, i studierte

2

a Die Karten kosteten nichts.

b Wir wohnten im Ausland.

c Ich hörte ein Geräusch.

d Die Mädchen lachten laut.

e Es regnete gestern.

f Wir warteten auf den Zug.

The imperfect tense: strong verbs, mixed verbs (page 28)

1

2

a standen, b empfahl, c fingen, d gewann, e half, f sangen, g nahm, h taten, i lief, j sahen

The genitive case (page 29)

1

a Die Katze meiner Freundin ist schwarz und weiß.

b Am Ende des Konzerts gingen wir nach Hause.

c Das Porträt eines Musikers hing in der Galerie.

d Das Zimmer meiner Schwester sieht immer so ordentlich aus.

e Ich habe nur die ersten zwei Seiten des Romans gelesen.

f Wir konnten die Mutter der Kinder nicht finden.

g Sie hat ein Bild eines Autos gezeichnet.

h Man konnte die Namen der Schauspielerinnen nicht lesen.

2

a wegen des Internets

b anstatt eines Handys

c während der Werbepause

d trotz der Probleme

e wegen des Wetters

f während des Sommers

Comparative and superlative adjectives (page 30)

1

a länger, b größte, c schöner, d nächste, e späteste, f netter, g schnellste, h vernünftiger, i ärmste, j lustiger

2

a schnellsten, b beste, c schönsten, d höchsten, e nächste, f intelligenteste

3

These are suggestions only.

a Bayern München ist besser als Chelsea.

b Salat ist gesünder als Pommes frites.

c Venedig ist schöner als Paris.

d 'Skyfall' ist spannender als 'Avatar'.

4

Based on the above suggested answers.

a Chelsea ist nicht so gut wie Bayern München.

b Pommes frites sind nicht so gesund wie Salat.

c Paris ist nicht so schön wie Venedig.

d 'Avatar' ist nicht so spannend wie 'Skyfall'.

5

Students' own answers.

Modal verbs (page 31)

a darf, **b** sollst, **c** mögen, **d** will, **e** müsst, **f** können, **g** soll, **h** Kann

2
a
I have had to write a letter.
He has been allowed to go home.
We have been able to swim every day.
Didn't your friends want to come along?

b
Ich habe einen Brief schreiben müssen.
Er hat nach Hause gehen dürfen.
Wir haben jeden Tag schwimmen können.
Haben deine Freunde nicht mitkommen wollen?

Mein Neffe hat gestern Abend nicht fernsehen dürfen.
Wir haben heute ins Theater gehen wollen.
Ich habe den Arzt anrufen müssen.
Hast du das Schild nicht lesen können?

Possessive adjectives (page 32)

a Mein, seinen, **b** meiner, ihr, **c** Seine, ihr, **d** Mein, meinem, **e** sein, unserer, mein, **g** ihrer, **h** seinem, unsere

2 unser, **b** Mein, ihrer, **c** unseren, meinem, **d** eure, **e** Meine, unserer, Unsere, ihre, **g** seiner, seinen, **h** Ihre, unseren, **i** Unsere, dein, mein, seiner

Word order (page 33)

Zu Ostern haben wir eine Woche in Wien verbracht.
Bald wird mein Cousin in die Schweiz fliegen.
Heute bin ich zum ersten Mal mit der Straßenbahn gefahren.
Auf dieser Autobahn gibt es jeden Tag einen Stau.
Er ist während der Ferien mit seinen Freunden im See geschwommen.
Danach habe ich meine Freunde in der Stadtmitte getroffen./
Danach habe ich in der Stadtmitte meine Freunde getroffen.

Markus sieht gern Filme, aber er geht nicht so oft ins Kino.
Ich weiß nicht, wann der Zug abfährt.
Willst du immer noch ausgehen, obwohl es heute so kalt ist?
Er hat nicht gehört, was sie gesagt hat.
Die Kinder sind sofort nach Hause gegangen, denn sie wollten mit ihrem Hund spielen.
Wir haben uns noch nicht entschieden, wie lange wir auf dem Campingplatz bleiben werden.

Forming questions (page 34)

Ruft mein Onkel heute Abend an?
Könnte sie den Brief nicht lesen?
Ist das Paket für mich schon angekommen?
Hast du ihn gestern Vormittag gesehen?
Darf sein Bruder keine Erdnüsse essen?
Sind Ilse und ihre Familie noch einen Tag geblieben?
Muss man dieses lange Formular ausfüllen?
Fängt das Konzert um halb acht an?

These are suggestions only.
Wie lange möchten Sie in Deutschland arbeiten?
Hast du diese Sendung gesehen?
Warum kauft sie ein neues Auto?
Wo wird der Film gedreht?
Wer ist sie?
Fand das Musikfestival letzte Woche statt?

3
Students' own answers.

Nominative, accusative and dative cases (page 35)

1
a Er kommt nächsten Freitag.
b Der Wein kostet 20 € die Flasche.
c Wir sind eine Nacht geblieben.
d Das Baby ist erst einen Monat alt.
e Wir kauften/haben das Auto letzten Februar gekauft.
f Jeden Mittwoch besucht sie ihren Opa.

2
a dir – Have you sprained your ankle?
b dem – I was very grateful to the doctor.
c ihrer – Birgit is similar to her mother.
d ihm – He didn't know of this woman.
e ihr – A stranger saved her life.

3
a Mir ist so kalt. **b** Es tut uns Leid. **c** Es ist ihm egal.
d Ihnen ist warm.

Mixed practice (page 36)

1
a meiner, dieses, meinem, **b** den, einen, **c** Letzten, den,
d Ihre, der, ihrem, **e** unseres Aufenthalts, der, einen,
f des Regens, keinen, **g** Das, die, die

2
a längste, **b** schlimmste, **c** erfolgreichste, **d** höchste, **e** jüngste,
f beste

3
gab, wurde, konnte, sah, hatte, war, brachte, untersuchte, musste, durfte

Test yourself (page 37)

1
a komponierte, **b** wollen, **c** gefällt/gefiel, **d** brachten, **e** genieße,
f anziehe, **g** kam, starb, **h** wird, **i** sollte, **j** aussahen

2
a iii, **b** iii, **c** ii, **d** i, **e** ii, **f** ii, **g** i, **h** iii

Topic 3
Modal verbs (page 38)

1
a I, **b** S, **c** IS, **d** S, **e** I, **f** IS, **g** I, **h** S, **i** S, **j** IS

2
a dürfte – Gabi would be allowed to go the cinema.
b könnten – Perhaps we could/would be able to meet later.
c möchten – My friends would like to come along.
d müsste – How hard would I have to train?
e möchte – From tomorrow I'd like to exercise regularly.
f könntet – When could you/would you be able to come round?

3
a musste, **b** könnten, **c** möchte, **d** konntest, **e** durften, **f** könnte

The infinitive with zu (page 39)

1
a –, **b** –, **c** zu, **d** zu, **e** –, **f** zu, **g** zu, **h** –

2
a um ein Hemd zu kaufen.
b ohne zu viel Geld zu verschwenden.
c anstatt fernzusehen.
d um alles zu verstehen.
e anstatt die Polizei zu rufen.
f ohne die Haustür abzuschließen.

Subordinate clauses and subordinating conjunctions (page 40)

1

a Ich habe eine Stunde gewartet, bis sie nach Hause gekommen ist.

b Sie können mich einfach anrufen, falls es Probleme gibt.

c Der Skateboardfahrer brach den Weltrekord, indem er über eine 25 Meter lange Grube sprang.

d Meine Freundinnen treiben nicht genug Sport, obwohl sie fit werden wollen.

2

a Bis sie nach Hause gekommen ist, habe ich eine Stunde gewartet.

b Falls es Probleme gibt, können Sie mich einfach anrufen.

c Indem er über eine 25 Meter lange Grube sprang, brach der Skateboardfahrer den Weltrekord.

d Obwohl sie fit werden wollen, treiben meine Freundinnen nicht genug Sport.

3

a seitdem wir unser Haus verkauft haben.

b sobald die Schule aus war.

c damit die Menschen gesund bleiben?

d Falls du Schwierigkeiten hast,

e solange er den Computer benutzen darf.

f Obwohl sein Handy nicht sehr alt ist,

Key subjunctive forms (page 41)

1

a wäre, würde, **b** würdest, hättest, **c** würde, gäbe, **d** gäbe, würden, **e** würde, hätte, **f** hätte, könnte, **g** wäre, hätte, **h** dürften, wäre

2

Suggested answers.

a Wenn ich mehr Zeit hätte, würde ich den Tag am Strand verbringen.

b Wenn es keine illegalen Drogen mehr gäbe, wäre das toll.

c Wenn er schlanker wäre, würde er sich mehr bewegen.

d Wenn ich reich wäre, würde ich den armen Menschen in Afrika helfen.

3

a Sie hätte gekauft.

b Sie wären gewesen.

c Wir wären geblieben.

d Meine Eltern hätten angerufen.

e Ich hätte geschrieben.

f Er wäre weggegangen.

g Hättest du gefragt?

h Wir wären angekommen.

Relative pronouns (page 42)

1

a den – That is the belt (which/that) she bought yesterday.

b dessen – The football player whose arm was broken had to go to hospital.

c der – She found a ring which/that is very valuable.

d die – The people who live next to us are very friendly.

e der – The lady to whom I was speaking/The lady I was speaking to is my former English teacher.

f die – Alcohol is a drug which/that is often misused.

2

Suggested answers.

a Der Film, den wir letzte Woche gesehen haben, war ausgezeichnet.

b Der Junge, dessen Fahrrad gestohlen wurde, war richtig böse.

c Die Häuser, in denen die Leute wohnten, waren verfallen.

d Sie hat den Mann, den sie letztes Jahr in Spanien kennen lernte, vor kurzem geheiratet.

e Das Sofa, auf dem der Hund lag, ist jetzt schmutzig.

f Der Garten, in dem wir saßen, hatte einen Teich.

3

Students' own answers.

The imperative (page 43)

1

a Kommt, **b** Warten Sie, **c** Setz dich, **d** Bringen Sie, **e** Seid, **f** Mach

2

a Bleib! Bleibt! Bleiben Sie!

b Antworte! Antwortet! Antworten Sie!

c Wasch dich! Wascht euch! Waschen Sie sich!

d Nimm! Nehmt! Nehmen Sie!

3

a Ruf mich um 6 Uhr an!

b Nehmen Sie jetzt die Tabletten!

c Schaltet den Computer aus!

d Lies die Zeitschrift!

e Räum dein Zimmer auf!

Adjectival nouns (page 44)

1

a Der Obdachlose, **b** einer Erwachsenen, **c** den Armen, **d** der Drogensüchtigen, **e** Die Blinde, **f** Bekannte, **g** Behinderte, **h** dem Gefangenen

2

a Eine Deutsche, **b** die Erwachsenen, **c** einer Kranken, **d** einem Verwandten, **e** ein Blinder, **f** eine Obdachlose, **g** den Jugendlichen **h** Ein Behinderter

3

a Das Gute, **b** das Schlimmste, **c** Das Wichtigste, **d** das Innere

The subjunctive in conditional sentences (page 45)

1

a hätte, **b** käme, **c** wären, **d** wärest, **e** dürften, **f** müsste, **g** gäbe

Not used: wüsste

2

i würde, **ii** würdet, **iii** würde, **iv** würden, **v** würden, **vi** würde, **vii** würdest

3

Suggested answers as there may be more than one correct combination.

a **iii** (Example) Wenn ich ein schnelleres Auto hätte, würde ich meine Freunde bestimmt beeindrucken.

b **ii** Wenn euer Zug nicht pünktlich käme, würdet ihr den Anschlusszug verpassen.

c **v** Wenn sie nicht so schüchtern wären, würden meine Schwester mehr Freunde kennen lernen.

d **vii** Wenn du nicht so ungeduldig wärest, würdest du eine nette Person sein.

e **iv** Wenn unsere Freundinnen nicht mitkommen dürften, würde wir enttäuscht sein.

f **vi** Wenn ich beim Abspülen helfen müsste, würde es mir egal sein.

g **i** Wenn es keine Markenkleidung gäbe, würdest du nicht so viel Geld ausgeben.

4

Students' own answers.

Particles: doch, ja, mal, schon (page 46)

1

Suggested answers only.

a mal, **b** ja/doch, **c** schon, **d** ja, **e** doch, **f** schon, **g** doch, **h** mal, **i** ja **j** schon

Expressions of time (page 47)

1

a Eines Tages, **b** vier Tage, **c** eine Woche, **d** seit einem Jahr, **e** eines Morgens, **f** Vor drei Jahren, **g** sechs Monate, **h** für zehn Tage

nach einer Woche, **b** in zwei Studen, **c** während des Frühlings,
um Mitternacht, **e** am Freitag, **f** am Abend, **g** zu/an Ostern,**h** eines
achts, **i** bis nächsten Mittwoch, **j** vor einem Jahr, **k** vor der Reise,
eit letzter Woche, **m** gegen zehn Uhr, **n** am 3. Mai

ixed practice (page 48)

Was würdest du machen, wenn du kein Handy hättest?
Ohne ein einziges Wort zu sagen, hat sie das Zimmer verlassen.
Kommen Sie morgen vorbei, wenn Sie Zeit haben.
Anstatt eine SMS zu schicken, hat er eine E-Mail geschickt.
Wir wären ins Konzert gegangen, wenn wir Karten gehabt hätten.
Bleib hier, wenn du willst.
Wir wollen ins Kino gehen, um den neuesten Actionfilm zu sehen.
Seid doch ruhig!

önnten, **b** musste, **c** möchten, **d** konnte, **e** könntest, **f** durfte,
onnte, **h** dürfte

er, **b** der, **c** den, **d** der, **e** die, **f** dem, **g** das, **h** deren

xed practice (page 49)

, **b** F, **c** T, **d** NA, **e** T, **f** F

ann wurde eigentlich die Fernsehfernbedienung erfunden?
s ist lange her. Die Fernbedienung gab es Mitte der 50er Jahre
ne Kabel. Da der DVD-Spieler, der Videorekorder und der
tellitenempfänger eine eigene Fernbedienung haben müssen ist
wischen das ganze Wohnzimmer voll damit. Und der Fernseher
d immer schlauer: Man kann Fotos anschauen, spielen oder im
ernet surfen.
eil man mit der Fernbedienung keine Internetadresse schreiben
nn sind die Tage der Fernbedienung gezählt. Und wie sollen
in Zukunft den Fernseher bedienen? Indem wir mit ihm reden
d ihm Zeichen geben. Anfang des Jahres wurde auf der weltweit
ßten Messe für Unterhaltungselektronik in Las Vegas ein solcher
nseher vorgestellt – mit Sprach- und Gestenbedienung.
r neue Fernseher hat Augen und Ohren oberhalb des Bildschirms.
mera und Mikrofon können uns sehen und hören. Statt den
nseher einzuschalten, reicht einfach eine Begrüßung, z. B. „'n
end Fernseher". Wenn man das Programm wechseln will genügt
„Kanal wechseln, Kanal 4". Und falls man keine Lust hat, mit
n Fernseher zu reden, reicht auch eine Handbewegung.
nn gibt es diesen neuen Fernseher zu kaufen? Ab Ende März. Der
is liegt zwischen 1500 € und 3000 €, je nach Größe. Nur eins ist
igens unklar: Wie soll der Fernseher meine Gesten im Dunkeln
en? Dann kann man ja mit ihm reden!

st yourself (page 50)

Timo/Andreas, **b** Jennifer, **c** Andreas, **d** Sebastian, **e** Katharina,
Daniela

Andreas) Um wie die Stars auszusehen
Timo) um für andere attraktiv auszusehen
m sich einfach besser zu fühlen
m nach außen gut rüberzukommen
Jennifer) Um intelligent zu sein
Sebastian) Um erfolgreich zu sein

ch brauche mindestens eine Stunde, um mich für die Arbeit
ertig zu machen./Um mich für die Arbeit fertig zu machen,
rauche ich mindestens eine Stunde.

Test yourself (page 51)

2
a wohnt, **b** hätte, **c** durfte, **d** produziert, **e** mussten, **f** iss, **g** würden,
h wollte, **i** wären, hätten, **j** müsste

3
a viele Arme, **b** Die Gefangenen, **c** der Obdachlosen,
d Ein Verwandter, **e** einem Bekannten, **f** Die Drogensüchtige,
g die Jugendlichen, **h** Erwachsenen, **i** Seine Verlobte,
j keine Überlebenden

Topic 4
Infinitives (page 52)

1
a intransitive verb (a verb not used with a direct object, e.g.
  sterben)
b separable verb (a verb with a separable prefix, e.g. ankommen)
c transitive verb (a verb used with a direct object, e.g. kaufen)
d irregular verb (a verb not following the pattern of a weak or
  strong verb, e.g. kennen)
e reflexive verb (a verb used with a reflexive pronoun, e.g. sich
  waschen)
f inseparable verb (a verb with a prefix which is never removed,
  e.g. versuchen)
g auxiliary verb (a verb used with a past participle, e.g. haben)

2
a transitive, inseparable verb
  Der Arzt untersucht mich.
b inseparable, intransitive verb, someone/something + dative
  Sie widersprechen ihm immer.
c transitive, separable, irregular verb
  Du nimmst es als selbstverständlich hin.
d transitive, separable, irregular verb, someone + dative
  Er bringt euch Italienisch bei.
e irregular, transitive verb, someone + dative, omit 'for' in German
  here
  Ich werde dir den Unfall vergeben.
f transitive, inseparable verb, someone + accusative
  Der Lkw hat ihn überfahren./Der Lkw überfuhr ihn.
g intransitive, separable verb, auxiliary verb = sein, used with
  dative
  Sie ist mir entgegengelaufen./Sie lief mir entgegen.
h separable, irregular, reflexive verb
  Sie haben sich schnell umgezogen./Sie zogen sich schnell um.
i reflexive verb, 'to' someone = von + dative
  Wir haben uns von unseren Freunden verabschiedet./Wir
  verabschiedeten uns von unseren Freunden.
j transitive verb, someone = 'bei' + dative
  Sie hat bei ihr den Eindruck erweckt, dass .../Sie erweckte bei ihr
  den Eindruck, dass ...

Possessive adjectives (page 53)

1
a deiner, **b** eure, **c** meinen, meinem, **d** seiner, ihr, **e** ihre, **f** unserer

2
a in meinem Leben, **b** für seinen Onkel, **c** nach unserer Pause,
d während ihres Aufenthalts, **e** von deiner Schwester, **f** gegenüber
ihrem Haus, **g** anstatt ihres Kulis, **h** ohne seinen Fotoapparat/seine
Kamera, **i** mit Ihren Hunden, **j** seit ihrem Unfall

3
a Mein, deiner, **b** meinem, mein, mein, **c** deinem, seine, **d** Seine,
seiner, **e** Meinen, **f** ihrem, seine, **g** unserer, **h** eurem, **i** meiner, **j** Ihrer

The pluperfect tense (page 54)

1

a hatten – Fortunately, we hadn't missed the bus.

b hatte – I had decided to do the first aid course.

c war – Brigitte had gone swimming in the lake although the weather was very cold.

d hatte – It had started snowing, but we didn't mind.

e war – I had just gone to bed when the phone rang.

2

a Nachdem er den Brief gelesen hatte, rief er mich an.

b Nach der Überfahrt hatte ich mich krank gefühlt.

c Meine Freundin war noch nie im Ausland gewesen, also machten wir einen Tagesausflug nach Frankreich.

d Nach den Examen waren meine Freunde in Urlaub gefahren.

e Ich hatte versucht, sie anzurufen, aber leider hatte sie das Haus schon verlassen.

f Bevor meine Familie und ich nach Deutschland kamen, war meine Oma leider gestorben.

g Da es viel kälter geworden war, wollten wir nicht ausgehen.

3

a The house had been damaged by an explosion.

b Unfortunately, the jewels had never been found.

c 100 years ago the mobile telephone had not yet been invented.

Adjectival endings (page 55)

1

a kleine, großen, b neuen, c alte, kleinen, d junge, blauen, e ältere, jüngere, f langen, schönsten

2

a alten, hübschen, b bester, gebrauchtes, c großen, kleiner, schönen, d guten, e schweren, langen, f modernen, tolle, g langen, deutschen, h nettes, interessanten

Adjectival endings (continued) (page 56)

3

a Brasilianischer, b schlechtes, c moderne, d französischen, e gekochte, f gemähtem, g spanische, h europäischen, i grünen, frische, j kurzer, indische

4

a nichts Kaltes, b etwas Kleines, c wenig Interessantes, d viel Wichtiges

5

a österreichische, romantische, b langen, große, c jüngster, rohes, d kleinen, ausländische, Interessantes, e alte, linken, f festen, schrecklichen, g Mögliche, besten, h schönen, alten, japanische, exotische, i reiche, amerikanischen, teure, j neuen, kleinen

The future perfect tense (page 57)

1

a Dieses Wochenende werden meine Eltern aus dem Urlaub zurückgekommen sein.

b Bis morgen Nachmittag wird man unseren neuen Kühlschrank geliefert haben.

c Durch dieses Training werden wir in sechs Wochen fünf Kilo abgenommen haben.

d Bis nächstes Jahr werde ich einen guten Job bekommen haben.

a My parents will have returned from holiday this weekend.

b Our new fridge will have been delivered by tomorrow afternoon.

c With this training we shall have lost 5 kilos in six weeks.

d By next year I shall have got a good job.

2

a Morgen um diese Zeit wirst du hoffentlich deine Fahrprüfung bestanden haben.

b Mein Chef wird meine E-Mail schon bekommen haben.

c Nach 20 Jahren werden sich viele Dinge geändert haben.

d Innerhalb von sechs Jahren werde ich vielleicht Pilot geworden sein.

e Die Lehrerin wird wahrscheinlich nach Hause gegangen sein.

f Wirst du bis Montag den Roman ausgelesen haben?

3

a Du wirst dieses Lied schon gehört haben.

b Bis morgen wird er in Tokio angekommen sein.

c Wir werden große Fortschritte gemacht haben.

d Bis nächstes Jahr wird man/werden sie eine Lösung gefunden haben.

The conditional and conditional perfect (page 58)

1

a sein, b haben, c sein

2

a Seine Mutter hätte ihn ins Krankenhaus gebracht.

b Wegen des Gewitters wäre ich lieber zu Hause geblieben.

c Meine Verwandten wären gestern vorbeigekommen.

d Hättet ihr den Obdachlosen geholfen?

a His mother would have taken him to hospital.

b Because of the storm I would have preferred to stay at home.

c My relatives would have called by yesterday.

d Would you have helped the homeless people?

3

a Sie würden länger trainiert haben.
  Sie hätten länger trainiert.

b Es würde nie passiert sein.
  Es wäre nie passiert.

c Ich würde ihnen eine SMS geschickt haben.
  Ich hätte ihnen eine SMS geschickt.

d Meine Oma würde hingefallen sein.
  Meine Oma wäre hingefallen.

Subjunctive 1 (page 59)

1

a S, b IS, c I, d IS, e S, f S, g S, h IS, i S, j I

2

a fühle, b wohne, c gebe, d treffe, e heirate, f mache

3

a Der Junge sagte, er habe den Ball verloren.

b Meine Mutter sagte uns, sie habe einen Kuchen gebacken.

c Vati sagte, er sei am Freitag nach Stuttgart gefahren.

d Man sagte, sie sei eine berühmte Schauspielerin geworden.

e Der Direktor sagte, er habe gerade mit meinen Eltern gesprochen.

f Ihr Bruder sagte, er sei erst um 13 Uhr aufgestanden.

g Meine Schwester sagte, unsere Oma sei im Sessel eingeschlafe

h Der Mann sagte, er habe seinen Hund nicht gefunden.

Subjunctive 2 (page 60)

1

a schliefen, b schickte, c käme, d ginge, e wäre, f wüsstest, g würden, h kauftet, i hätte, j gäbe

2

a komme, b kämen, c schreibe, d hätten, e habe, f habe … gesehe
g hätten … gemacht, h sei … ausgegangen

3

a Sie sahen aus, als ob sie unglücklich wären.

b Er sah aus, als ob er seit Tagen nicht gegessen hätte.

c Sie sahen aus, als ob sie kein Geld hätten.

d Sie tat, als ob sie es eilig hätte.

e Der Mann tat, als ob nichts geschehen wäre.

Impersonal expressions (page 61)

1

a 5 Es liegt an seiner Hartnäckigkeit.

b 2 Es handelt sich um einen Mordfall in der Karibik.

c 6 Es gilt, Mut zu zeigen.

d 1 Es geht um Leben und Tod.

e 3 Es gibt keinen Grund dafür.

7 Es gefällt mir, am Strand zu liegen.
9 Es heißt, die Zeit heilt alle Wunden.
4 Es steht gut um sie.
8 Es fehlt mir an nichts.

It's due to his stubbornness.
It's about a murder case in the Caribbean.
It's necessary to show courage.
It's a matter of/It's about life and death.
There is no reason for it.
I like to lie on the beach.
It is said time heals all wounds.
Things are looking good for her.
I lack for nothing.

Es gefällt ihm, ins Kino zu gehen.
Es gelingt mir, das Abendessen zuzubereiten.
Es gilt, den Euro zu retten.
Es gelang uns/ist uns gelungen, einen Parkplatz zu finden.
Es gefiel ihr/hat ihr gefallen, ihre Großeltern zu besuchen.
Es gelang ihnen/ist ihnen gelungen, ihn zu erreichen.

ixed practice (page 62)

anfangen, **b** beibringen, **c** ausgehen, **d** springen, **e** einladen,
gelingen, **g** einschlafen, **h** bieten

Meine Mutter hatte ihr Portemonnaie völlig vergessen.
Er sagte, er sehe nicht gern fern.
Nachdem unsere Verwandten abgefahren waren, gingen wir ins Bett.
Wir würden ins Konzert gehen, wenn wir Karten hätten.
Die Kinder sagten, sie seien sehr müde.
Der Alte tat, als ob er krank wäre.
Sie sagten, sie müssten später zurückkommen.
Weil wir den letzten Bus verpasst hatten, mussten wir ein Taxi nehmen.

Ich hätte nie daran gedacht.
Er sagte, er habe den Film schon gesehen.
Mittlerweile wird mein Verlobter in Kanada angekommen sein.
Sie geht zum Zahnarzt, ohne einen Termin zu machen.
Um seinen Sohn zu trösten, hatte er ihm eine Geschichte erzählt.
Die Alte sah aus, als ob sie obdachlos wäre.

Mixed practice (page 63)

4a
A sein, zusammenbleiben, **B** zusammenleben, **C** heiraten,
D weglaufen, stellen, tragen, üben, **E** machen, **F** kennen lernen,
herauszufinden, **G** –

4b
zusammenbleiben, zusammenleben, weglaufen, kennenlernen,
herausfinden

4c
paragraphs + titles:
1E, 2G, 3B, 4F, 5C, 6A, 7D or in order of text, A6, B3, C5, D7, E1,
F4

Test yourself (page 64)

1a
a (Leo) guter, kleinen, ideale
 (Marion) gute, motorischen, neue
 (Richard) wichtigen, konsequente, festgesetzten, ideale
 (Sara) perfekte, finanziellen, alleiniger, ideale, große

1b
a Sara, **b** Richard, **c** Leo, **d** Sara, **e** Richard, **f** Marion

Test yourself (page 65)

2
a richtigen, **b** traditioneller, **c** kleine, **d** asiatischen, **e** hatten, **f** wäre,
g gelassen, **h** könntest, **i** gelöst, **j** gestiegen
3
a schlechten, **b** heutigen, **c** gute, **d** neuer, **e** erkannt, **f** wolle, **g** wäre,
h hatte, **i** müsste, **j** hätte

■ Acknowledgements

The author and the publisher would like to thank and acknowledge the following for the use of their material:

p.49 Wie zieht die Zukunft des Fernsehens aus? Adapted from: http://www.ndr.de/fernsehen/sendungen/mein_nachmittag/videos/zukunftfernsehen103.html, accessed 13 February 2013.

p.50 Ist Schönheit wichtig? Adapted from: Verbundschule Hille, http://www.verbundschulehille.de, accessed 13 February 2013.

p.63 Das große Zögern (Die Ehe), adapted from: http://www.sueddeutsche.de/leben/pro-und-contra-heirat-das-grosse-zoegern-1.710869, accessed 13 February 2013.

p.64 Was zeichnet einen guten Vater aus? (Wer ist der beste Vater?) Adapted from: http://www.netmoms.de/magazin/familie/familienleben/was-zeichnet-einen-guten-vater-aus?, accessed 13 February 2013.

Every effort has been made to trace the copyright holders but if any have been inadvertently overlooked the publisher will be pleased to make the necessary amendments or arrangements at the first opportunity.

Practise and Performance Tips

Before you begin, here are some practise tips to help you maximise your study time and progress. These outline a way to organise your time that I've found effective for players of any level.

To progress quickly, it's essential to be as regular and productive with your practice time as possible. To do this, you must identify the sections of your study piece that are the most difficult. These could be a single chord shape, a sequence of hammer-ons and pull-offs, or a picking hand pattern.

Take these challenging passages and practise each one in isolation for a short period of time. Focus on being slow, accurate and relaxed. It's tempting to continue after the point of difficulty, especially when reading from a book, so it may help to copy the trouble-spots out onto a separate piece of tab paper to prevent you from getting distracted.

If you have twenty minutes to practise one piece, I suggest you allot fifteen minutes to about five tricky sections. Play each one for a minute in turn (I set a timer on my phone) and repeat three times. This approach keeps you engaged and helps you retain the information more clearly.

The remaining five minutes should be spent playing the full piece, or as large a section as you're able to work through. Play at a speed where most of it feels comfortable. Don't worry too much about nailing the trouble spots, just concentrate on feeling the flow of the piece as a whole and rewarding yourself for your hard work by making music.

Maintain this two-pronged attack daily for a couple of weeks and you will have much better results than simply playing the pieces over and over again.

Throughout the book I suggest picking and fingering patterns. The convention is to refer to the picking hand fingers with the following letters: P (thumb), I (index), M (middle), A (ring). In the notation, the fretting hand will be noted with the numbers 1 to 4, going from the index to pinkie.

I will occasionally refer to playing in numerical positions on the fretboard. These are where the first finger rests, even if the focus is on another finger. For example, playing in the fourth position means the first finger is fretting the 4th fret.

The following pieces often sound good at several different tempos, so don't rush to build speed. Once you are feeling confident with a tune, experiment with tempo to express a range of moods.

Most of the audio tracks were recorded on a nylon string classical guitar, but a few were played with a steel-string acoustic guitar for some tonal variation.

Get the Audio

The audio files for this book are available to download for free from **www.fundamental-changes.com** and the link is in the top right corner. Simply select this book title from the drop-down menu and follow the instructions to get the audio.

We recommend that you download the files directly to your computer, not to your tablet, and extract them there before adding them to your media library. You can then put them on your tablet, iPod or burn them to CD. On the download page there is a help PDF and we also provide technical support via the contact form.

Kindle / eReaders

To get the most out of this book, remember that you can double tap any image to enlarge it. Turn off 'column viewing' and hold your kindle in landscape mode.

For over 250 Free Guitar Lessons with Videos Check out:

www.fundamental-changes.com

Twitter: @guitar_joseph

FaceBook: FundamentalChangesInGuitar

Instagram: FundamentalChanges

1. Study No. 1 – Fernando Sor

This study comes from Sor's Opus 35, entitled *Vingt Quatre Exercices très Faciles (Twenty-Four Easy Exercises)*, making it a great place to start your repertoire. Sor self-published the opus late in his career and the whole collection offers a set of well-balanced miniatures with plenty of contrast.

The first study sticks to a dependable rhythm of crotchets and minims, and the pitches fit mostly into open-position chord shapes. Noticing similarities between the familiar chord shapes will give you an increased awareness of the harmonic composition and make the piece easier to memorise. For example, the first two bars outline a C major chord and bar three centres around F major.

Notes should be held where possible, although the full chord shapes you should fret may not be immediately obvious.

If you're new to fingerstyle technique, one of the biggest challenges is to develop sufficient dexterity in your picking hand to keep independence between the thumb and fingers. Isolate any points where your thumb and a finger are needed simultaneously and practise the "pinching" motion to get them to connect accurately with the strings. The position of your hand shouldn't move far from where it normally rests over the strings.

There are two independent melodies in this piece. The top voice moves in crotchets for most of the piece, while the lower voice moves more slowly. The voices are switched towards the end of the piece, where the bassline becomes the faster part. The direction of the note tails in the notation show which line each note belongs to.

Study No. 1 - Fernando Sor

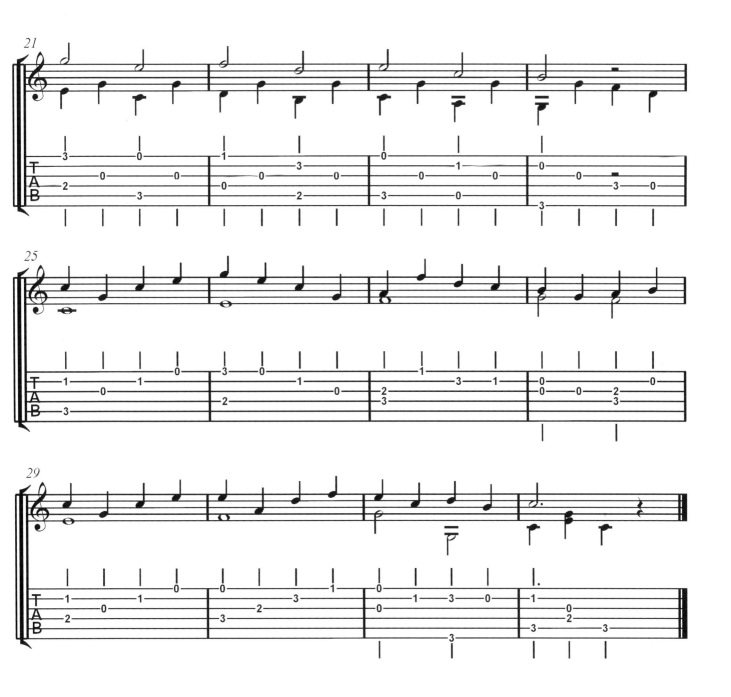

2. Country Dance – Ferdinando Carulli

Western classical music has its roots in traditional dances and military music. In the classical repertoire there are many gigues, mazurkas, minuets, polkas, waltzes, and marches from the era known as the *common-practice period* (roughly 1650-1900).

Musicians, however, have a way of subverting musical forms. I doubt you could dance to any of Chopin's waltzes! While the inspiration for this piece is dance music, and the best starting point is to keep an even tempo throughout, it's okay to be expressive and fluid with the tempo.

In Country Dance, the use of double-stops (two notes played simultaneously) allows us to easily alternate chords and bass notes. Your picking hand fingers should act as one, with two fingers fused together. Making an exercise out of the first two bars allows you to get this picking pattern "programmed" before worrying about the chord changes.

The third section requires a different picking pattern for the E minor chord in the first two bars. Rest the fingers of the picking hand (P, I, M and A) on the top four strings, then pluck each in turn with a smooth motion.

The structure needs some concentration to navigate. There are three sections, each of which is played twice. At the end of the piece, you will see the instruction *D.C. Al Fine*, which directs you back to the start. Continue until the Fine instruction located at the end of the second section. The form is described as A B C A B.

Again, look out for the familiar chord shapes – G, D7 and Em – that are found throughout.

Carulli picked up guitar relatively late, at 20 years old, but composed a lot of music, including many instructional pieces that have remained popular, as they combine effective learning with music that's satisfying to play. There are several more pieces by Carulli throughout the book.

Country Dance – Ferdinando Carulli

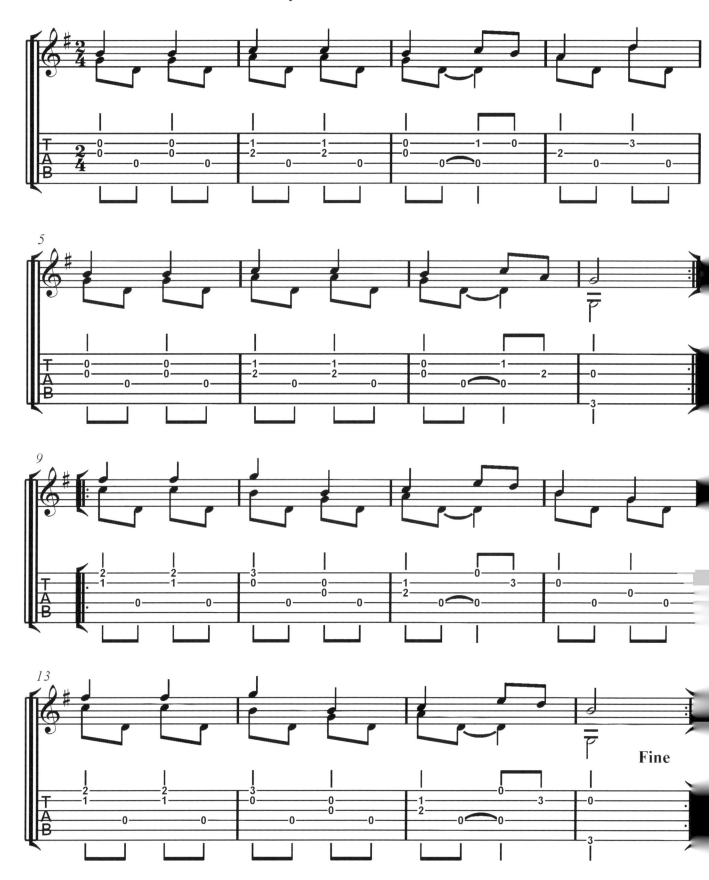

Fine

D.C. al fine

3. Orlando Sleepeth – John Dowland

John Dowland (1563-1626) was primarily a songwriter and lute player in Elizabethan England. He is best known for his rather maudlin songs and his instrumental compositions. This short piece has a repetitive folk music-esque melody that could easily have lyrics set to it, but works well as an instrumental study.

John Dowland either composed *Orlando Sleepeth*, or arranged an existing tune. It is also suggested that it was intended to be incidental music for a scene in a play.

If you are comfortable with common open chord-shapes, this piece shouldn't give you too much trouble. To help you understand the structure, identify the chord shapes as you work through the music and write them in the notation.

In bar two, instead of fretting the D Major chord in the usual manner, barre at the 2nd fret with your first finger. This will help your fourth finger to reach up to the 5th fret.

Similarly, the G Major chord at the end of bar nine should be played with your third and fourth fingers, which may be a new approach. Using your third finger to play the bass note allows for a much smoother transition to the C Major chord than the traditional G Major fingering.

With all the open strings it's easy to let each note ring out, but in order to present the melody with clarity, mute the open strings at the appropriate times. For example, in bar eleven, your picking hand should silence the open B string just as it picks the G# note on beat 4.

The most difficult element occurs as the piece changes from 4/4 to 6/4 in bar seventeen. 6/4 time is a *compound meter*, which means that the notes are grouped into threes rather than the usual twos. You may have encountered songs in 6/8, and 6/4 can be treated in the same way. Beats 1 and 4 are accented.

A common feature of music from this period is that the compound section accelerates. A symbol above the notation indicates one minim is equal to a dotted minim. This means that three beats in the new meter should take the same time as two beats from the original.

This can be awkward to count. Before you begin, clap along to the audio track on beats 1 and 3. Maintain this pulse as the piece moves into 6/4. The music should now fit three beats into each of your taps.

As you get used to hearing the transition, you will be able to accurately speed up by the appropriate amount.

Orlando Sleepeth – John Dowland

D.C. al Fine

4. Dance No. 2 from Twelve Ländler, Op. 44 – Mauro Giuliani

The *ländler* was a popular Germanic folk dance. Its roots are likely to have been a lively couples' dance with much stomping and hopping before it became gentrified in Austrian dance halls during the 19th century. The dominant first beat of each bar suggests it was a forerunner of the waltz.

This short piece by Giuliani is a great introduction to larger *position shifts*. Positions on the guitar refer to the location of the first finger of the fretting hand, even if it's not being used. For example, in the pickup bar you will be in 1st position until the middle of bar three. Use your second and then third finger to fret the notes at the 2nd fret before bringing down the first finger at the start of bar one.

There are more dramatic position shifts leading into bar four. The temptation might be to lurch up and down the fretboard with one finger, but using several fingers will minimise the amount of movement and give you more control. Notes on the E string should be divided into three positions. I've added fingerings over the notation to show which notes should be played with the first finger.

Carefully memorise the passage and pay particular attention to which frets the first finger moves to. Other practice methods, such as singing the tune or imagining yourself playing the order of notes, are effective ways to cement the sequence of notes. The position shifts will become much easier as you are able to confidently think ahead.

The second half of the piece superimposes the first section over new bass notes. One of the strengths of traditional notation is that a melodic shape is easy to see when you look at the shape of the line. Compare the two sections yourself to see the similarity between the two parts.

In bars ten to thirteen there are more position shifts, but here the melody doesn't split so easily into three-note chunks. Begin in the same way as the first section, but once you've played the 10th fret with your fourth finger in bar eleven, slide your fourth finger up to the 12th fret, where it will stay for the rest of the bar. Position shifts with fingers other than the first might feel strange, but stick with them as you'll further develop this skill later.

In bar twelve, move from the 9th to the 10th fret with your first finger. The longest position shift is between bars thirteen and fourteen. Thankfully, the open E string gives you extra time, but your third finger will need plenty of practise to reliably make the leap from the 9th to 4th fret.

Once your fretting hand is comfortable with the position shifts, turn your attention to your picking hand. In the notation the bass note in each bar is followed by two rests. To play the piece accurately you should bring your thumb to rest on the string to dampen each bass note on beat 2.

Dance No. 2 from Twelve Ländler, Op. 44 – Mauro Giuliani

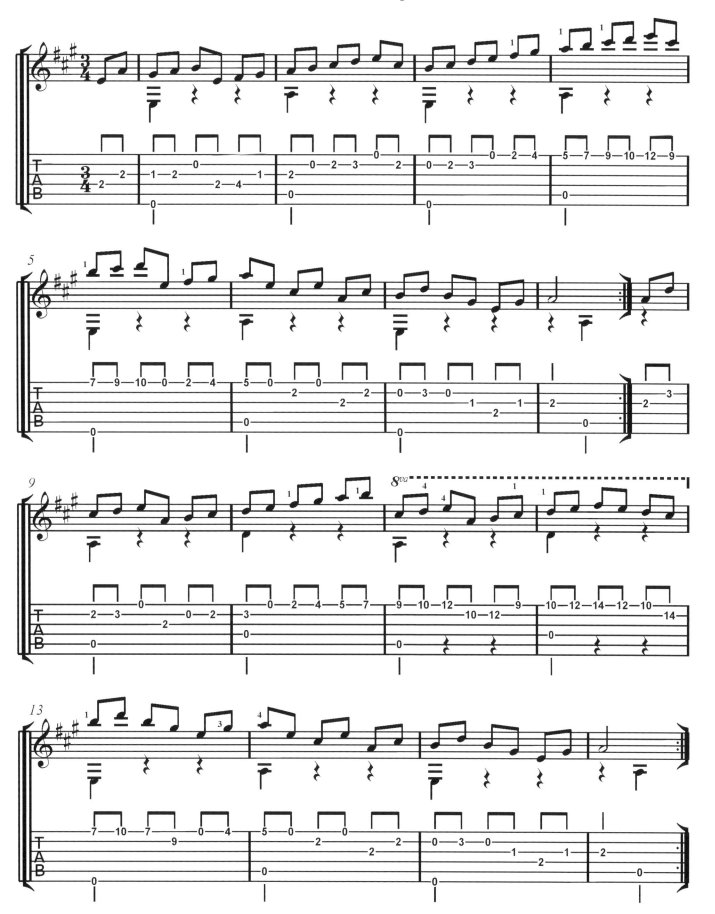

5. Study No. 2 – Fernando Sor

The Italian composer Fernando Sor was a contemporary of Carulli and was active in the late classical period (late 18th to early 19th century).

This piece starts before the first full bar. This is a *pickup beat*, or *anacrusis*, which anticipates the strong pulse played on the open A-string in beat 1. The convention when numbering bars is always to discount the pickup bar, so bar 1 is the first *full* bar.

Counting into the piece with "1, 2, 3, & 1" should help you get the correct timing. Listen to the audio to get a clearer understanding. This motif occurs many times throughout the composition as a pickup.

In this piece, double-stops move around and articulate the melody. You can pluck these in either of two ways. The first option is to assign your I, M and A fingers to the G, B and E strings respectively, and use the appropriate fingers for each pair of notes. The alternative is to move across the strings with your I and M fingers. Your thumb should always pluck the bass notes.

The passage that first occurs in bars five to six is best plucked with P, I and M. The thumb creates a different tone to the fingers, so playing the bass notes with your thumb throughout will make the piece sound more consistent.

Finally, there are some tricky embellishments towards the end of the piece. Bars twenty-one and twenty-five have grace notes (*acciaccaturas*). These should be squeezed in just before the main beat. In bar twenty-one the three strings should be plucked together, then a pull-off is used to sound the C note on the B-string as soon as possible. The acciaccatura shouldn't have a rhythmic value of its own.

Bar twenty-five should be handled in the same way, although here there is a more effusive three-note turn around to the target note of F. Use the first and fourth fingers to perform the hammer-ons and pull-offs. You will find it helpful to practise the top-string notes without playing the rest of the chord.

If the acciaccaturas prove too tricky at first, simply omit them. It won't detract much from the overall effect and you can add them in once you are comfortable with the technique.

As always, listen to the audio to hear how these techniques sound.

Study No. 2 – Fernando Sor

23

6. Andantino – Ferdinando Carulli

This piece will develop your picking hand, as well as teaching you a common sequence of *tenth* intervals (they are ten notes apart within the major scale) which often occur in classical guitar music. You were introduced to using multiple picking-hand fingers on alternating chords in the previous pieces and Andantino will further build your finger independence by alternating the fingers while maintaining a bass note.

The first bar contains low bass notes and alternating high notes. On the first beat, the G Major chord is arpeggiated. Your M and P fingers should pluck together with a pinching motion, followed by the I finger.

The melodic pick-up phrases, such as at the end of bar two, should be played by alternating two plucking fingers on one string. You might need to slightly change your hand position to allow both fingers to line up along the string.

The opening of the piece moves through a series of tenth intervals while maintaining a pedal tone of G.

In bars thirteen and fourteen, some of the bass note tails share a note with the melody. These notes form part of the melody, so stress them with a stronger pluck of your thumb to make the first and fourth semiquaver more pronounced.

Andantino – Ferdinando Carulli

7. Dance No. 6 from Twelve Ländler, Op. 44 – Mauro Giuliani

The sixth dance from Giuliani's set of twelve *ländlers* shares many features with the second. However, the emphasis here is on the lower register of the guitar.

The first section melody should be played with the thumb, until it moves onto the higher strings in bar four.

Next, some chordal ideas break up the flow. In bar five, the notes don't need to overlap, but the transition should be as smooth as possible. Keeping your thumb low on the back of the neck, and angling the neck vertically, will help make the stretch more manageable. Barre the 2nd fret with the first finger in bar six.

Bar seven contains a position shift similar to those in the earlier Giuliani *ländler*. Practise the bar slowly so that the joins between the fretted and open notes are smooth, but without too much overlap.

In the second section, the melody returns to the lower register. Combining the melody with the high chord fragments might seem difficult at first, but by using your second finger for the bass notes, the chords should soon fall into place with your first and fourth fingers. Slide the fourth finger up the B to start bar ten.

In bar ten the high notes should be played as a melody, rather than ringing together as a chord. To achieve this, alternate fingers four and three, rather than barring all the notes at the 7th fret.

To move back into the chord sequence, use your second finger for the D# in bar eleven. Pivot your hand on this note to prepare for the next chord.

In the final few bars the melody returns to the higher voice with some position shifting. By now, the fingering should be apparent.

These two pieces show how Giuliani developed two different compositions from a very similar starting point, by placing the melody in different registers and either making use of the harmony, or maintaining the sparse texture of a melody and a bassline. Once you've learnt both, they would combine well into one longer performance. Perhaps start with Dance No. 2, then No. 6, before returning to No. 2 again at the end.

Dance No. 6 from Twelve Ländler, Op. 44 – Mauro Giuliani

8. Waltz in E Minor – Ferdinando Carulli

One last Carulli piece for good measure! The Waltz in E Minor uses the approaches encountered so far in a slightly longer composition.

Smoothness is the most important quality when performing this piece, so play at a relaxed speed and allow each note ring for its full duration.

For example, the low E note in the first two bars should sound for the entire bar. Keep it held down with your first finger, before sliding that finger down to the 1st fret for bar three. To allow the notes to ring out, the fingers must come down from above, landing on their tips to avoid muting adjacent strings.

Similarly, the three fretted notes in bar nine should link together smoothly, rather than alternate with the open B-string. Play these notes without the top part at first, to see how smooth you can make it.

The second half of the piece alternates between double-stops and a rolling arpeggio figure. It can be tricky to move from one approach to the other without hesitation, so be sure to practise the transition at a very slow speed.

I always advocate cutting out small extracts from each piece to practise. This works well for bars seventeen and eighteen. Notice how the chord shape from beat 3 of bar seventeen is simply moved up two frets in the next bar. This position shift in the fretting hand should be performed in time, moving just as you pluck the D at the 3rd fret. The shape moves back down again for bar nineteen in the same fashion. Fretting hand fingers one and two should be used throughout.

9. Sweet William (Traditional)

This next piece departs from strictly "classical" music and draws on Irish folk. I wrote the arrangement especially for this book. It is quite straightforward in order to let the melody shine. Most of the accompaniment is long held bass notes.

Play each section of the piece with a confident and consistent tempo, but add some creative interpretation by allowing pauses between phrases.

Most of the fingering should be quite obvious, but note the first beat of bar ten. The G Minor fragment should be fingered with the third and fourth fingers to ensure a smooth transition from the pick-up notes in bar nine, and so that the following notes can be played comfortably with the first finger.

In bar sixteen, the bass notes should ring over the notes in between. Play the initial C Major fragment with your first and second fingers. Then keep the second finger held down while the first is replaced by the third, tucked under the second finger.

In the twenty-second bar your first finger can barre across the E and B strings throughout, with your third finger changing string at the 3rd fret as needed. This will avoid any gaps between the string changes and give the melody a more flowing and lyrical texture.

The harmony draws mostly on C Major, G Minor, and A Minor chords. Often the whole chord won't be used, but bits of familiar chord shapes crop up many times. If you can see which chord is being used, then you can develop this arrangement by plucking more notes in the chords to create a fuller sound.

Sweet William (Traditional)

10. Op. 1, Pt. 3, No. 1 – Mauro Giuliani

Giuliani was a multi-instrumentalist and composer, famed in his lifetime (1781-1829) as a virtuoso performer. This book has already introduced you to two pieces from his set of twelve *ländlers* (pages 17 & 24).

Aside from concert tours and composing, when living in Vienna Giuliani was a noted teacher. It's fitting that his first published work, Opus 1, is a comprehensive array of exercises broken down into chapters addressing specific elements of technique. It's still popular and well worth exploring for its wealth of warm-ups and technical exercises. It also contains several more musically satisfying études.

Part three of the work focuses on tone and articulation – and the next two selections are both drawn from it.

Apart from the occasional down-beat rest, the piece is a continuous melodic line, with a straight-forward bass accompaniment.

Giuliani's notes from the original publication stress the importance of the bass notes being held down for their full duration.

A good approach is to break the piece down into four-bar chunks and work through learning the melody then integrating the bass notes for those bars, before moving on. By keeping the chunks short, any short-sighted fingering choices in the melody won't become too ingrained.

Tackle the melodic line first without the bass accompaniment. Fingering will need to be carefully thought through once the bass notes are held down. For the most ergonomic fingering follow the numbers written over the notation.

Op. 1, Pt. 3, No. 1 – Mauro Giuliani

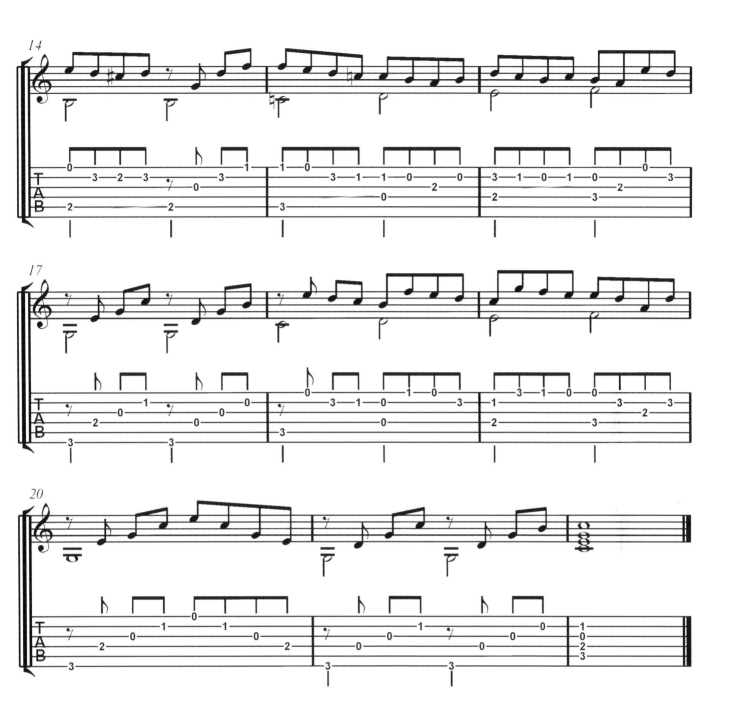

11. Op. 1, Pt. 3, No. 3 – Mauro Giuliani

The third piece from Giuliani's Op. 1 set of studies has more of a bouncing feel than the previous selection. Giuliani's own instructions state that the I and M fingers should pluck in a strictly alternating fashion to avoid fatigue developing in the right hand.

Carulli's Andantino (page 22) briefly uses this technique to play notes on a single string for short phrases, but here it is the subject of the whole study. Rest your thumb on the low E-string as an anchor point and play only the melody line until it's relaxed and accurate.

The rhythmic notation shows that each pair of notes is composed of a dotted semiquaver followed by a demisemiquaver. This rhythm may look a bit unnerving, but on listening to the audio, you will hear that the second note is delayed a bit, so that it rushes into the next strong beat. To produce these two quick notes, it is especially important to follow the picking instructions above.

The stated tempo is *allegro*, indicating that it should be played quite fast. However, I've played it at a more sedate tempo which gives the melody a bit more space. The strict plucking technique should be adhered to, so that with practise you will be able to play it at a range of tempos, as well as developing the technique needed for other pieces of a similar style.

Compare the two pieces from Giuliani's Op. 1 with the other classical period compositions and you'll notice that his phrases are much longer than most. While other pieces phrase in four-bar patterns, the melody in this piece doesn't really come to rest until the start of bar eight.

There are several pick-up beats in the tune, including the very first phrase. The eagle-eyed reader will spot that bar twelve is missing a quaver for the correct rhythmic value for a 2/4 bar. It was a convention of the period to repeat back to the start and include the pick-up bar again.

On the repetition, however, the pick-up counts as part of the preceding bar. After the second repeat at bar twelve, bar thirteen also has a pick-up which completes the previous bar's rhythmic value.

Op. 1, Pt. 3, No. 3 – Mauro Giuliani

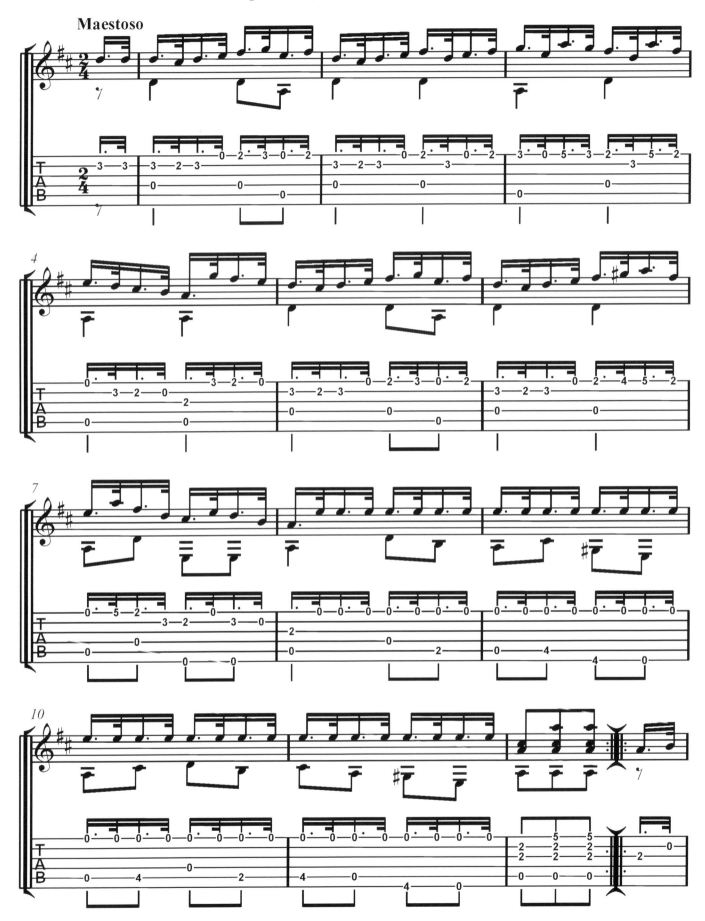

12. French Dance Op. 8 – Matteo Carcassi

Much like the other guitarists from the classical period covered so far, Matteo Carcassi (1792-1853) was born in Italy, but moved to Germany at age 18, before settling in Paris. He was equally renowned as a performer and a teacher.

Our first piece from Carcassi is from his Opus 8, *Etrennes aux Amateurs (New Pieces for Enthusiasts)*, which is a collection of various folk-inspired pieces, including French contra-dances, waltzes and airs. This is the first contra-dance.

The time signature at the start of the piece is 6/8, which means each bar contains six quavers, broken into two groups of three. The music should be felt in a triplet phrasing throughout, counting the six quavers in each bar as "1 & a, 2 & a".

I highlighted the use of tenth intervals in Carulli's Andantino, so you should be able to identify the same shapes in bars two and three. Having worked through several of the early pieces in the book, the first section shouldn't cause you any serious difficulties as many of those ideas are seen here.

The second section, which starts after the double barline in bar eight, has some tricky parts where your picking hand will need to be precise in plucking alternate strings using your P, I and A fingers. At the same time, your fretting hand is executing a variety of different pull-offs. Some of these are instant (those with small tails crossed out) and some are in time. Use the audio to hear how the part should sound.

The third section opens with an A Minor chord on the top strings, followed by an F Diminished chord. The chords can be plucked in a claw fashion, but given the quiet dynamic (notated by the *p* meaning *piano*, or softly), strumming them gently with the thumb might be more suitable.

The low single notes create a "call and response" with chords. The contrast between volume and attack should be maximised to make this part as dramatic and exciting as possible.

Following the climax there is a return to the first section, which can be calmer after the previous excitement. Slow down as you approach the end.

French Dance Op. 8 – Matteo Carcassi

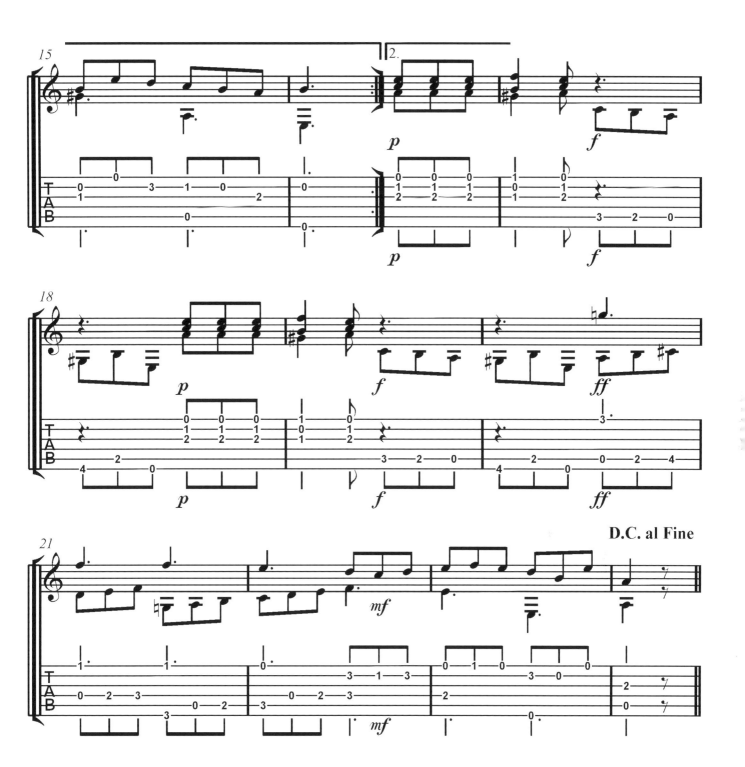

D.C. al Fine

13. Study in E Minor - Francisco Tárrega

Much like the other guitarists from the classical period covered so far, Matteo Carcassi (1792-1853) was born The Spanish composer Tárrega belongs in the Romantic era of music, being active in the late 19th century. His pieces are often programmatic, meaning they depict a non-musical subject, such as a scene or story. His most famous piece is *Recuerdos de la Alhambra* (Memories of the Alhambra), which was inspired by the Moorish architecture in Granada.

This short piece by Tárrega is an étude written to develop the plucking hand. The pattern is very consistent, so you can become familiar with it without worrying about too many variations.

Using your fourth finger to fret the G in bar one will allow the chord shapes in bars two and three to follow fluidly. Often, the best fingering only becomes apparent when you see where you need to move next. If you encounter a difficult section, look back to the previous bar and see if a different approach could make it easier.

Another such moment first occurs in bar nineteen. The D7 chord on beat 1 should be fingered conventionally, with the third finger on the top F# note. Add the fourth finger for the G melody note on beat 2, then slide it up to the 5th fret to build the third chord shape using the first and third fingers.

The final chord should be played as a harmonic. A harmonic makes a distinctive, pure bell-like tone. Lay the fretting hand finger across the 12th fret before plucking normally. The finger should just lightly touch the string. Make contact with the string directly over the metal frets, rather than between them. Remove the finger once the harmonic has been struck.

Standard finger-picking will work fine, but once you're comfortable you should investigate a technique called *rest stroke* to pluck the first note of each descending group. Rest stroke is where you pluck "across" the string and your finger comes to rest on the next string down. The normal practice of plucking by hooking slightly under the string and pulling out into space is known as *free stroke*.

Rest stroke gives a more forceful and strident sound, and will make the high note more pronounced. It gives the impression of a melody supported by a separate arpeggio accompaniment.

Study in E Minor - Francisco Tárrega

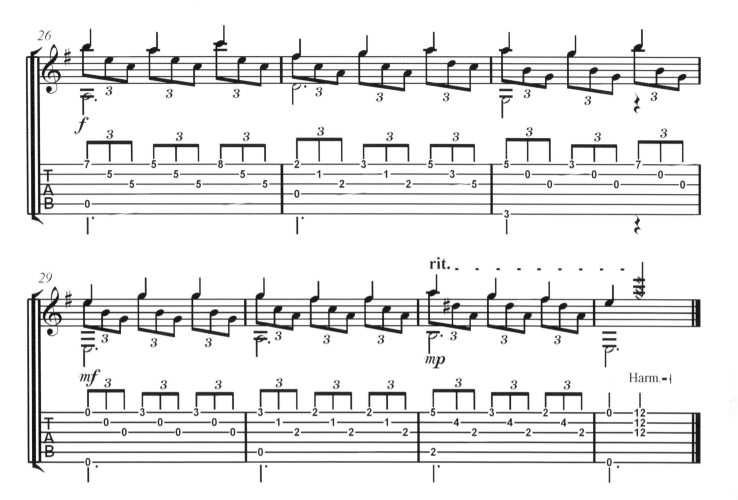

14. Andante in A Minor, Op. 241, No. 18 – Ferdinando Carulli

This short piece by Carulli comes from his later collection *École de Guitare* (Guitar School), published around 1825.

It presents a comprehensive method for tackling the technical challenges of the guitar music of his period. The picking patterns should be very familiar by now.

Take care that the single notes link up smoothly with the chord pattern. Alternate the plucking fingers when playing the scale parts. This may be confusing to start with, but will make things easier for your picking hand in the long run, so take it slowly for a while. Writing in the finger letters under the music (I, M or A) will help you practise consistently.

There is a subtle but important variation to the basic pattern in bar fifteen. The rhythm of the part is displaced, so that the chords are now on the off-beats. This variation adds a sense of tension as the music builds towards the end of the phrase. The effect is similar to speeding up, although the actual tempo remains the same. Follow the fingerings I've suggested for the final chord in bar fifteen.

Most of the second half of the piece should be very accessible as the tenth-based patterns have been well covered. However, there is one point, in bars twenty-eight and twenty-nine, where the best fingering may not be as obvious. I worked backwards from the middle of bar twenty-nine to avoid the fourth finger having to jump from the B-string to the D.

Listen to the audio to hear the intended tempo. You may find yourself racing ahead through the easier sections, but an *andante* is played at a tempo of 75-100bpm.

Once you can play it confidently at a fixed tempo, vary the phrasing during the second section (bars seventeen to thirty-seven). The end of each phrase is identified by a rest. Slow down as you approach each rest, then speed up again for the start of the next phrase.

Andante in A Minor, Op. 241, No. 18 – Ferdinando Carulli

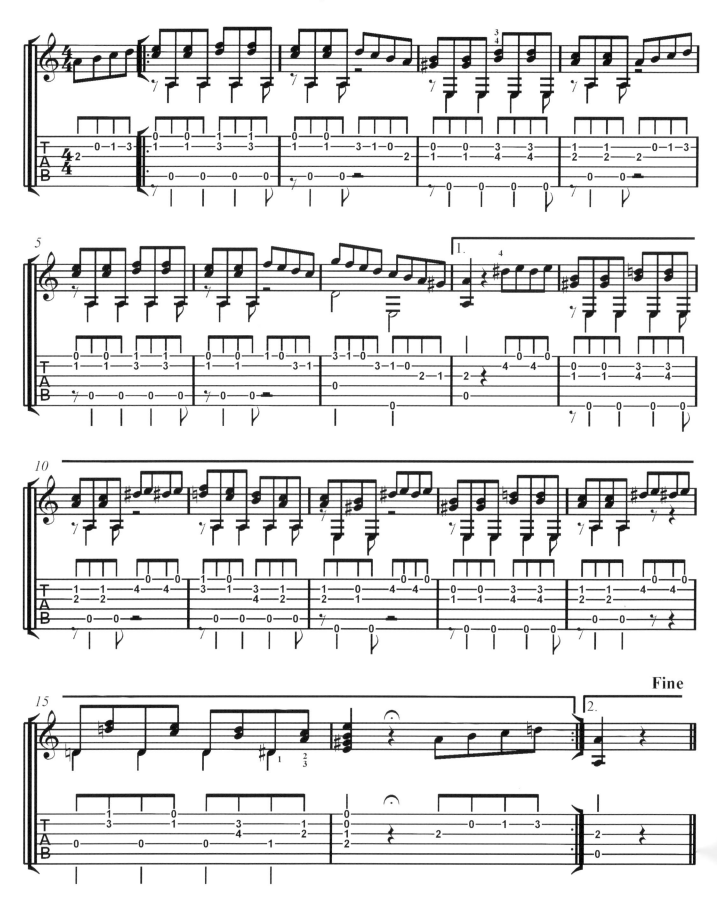

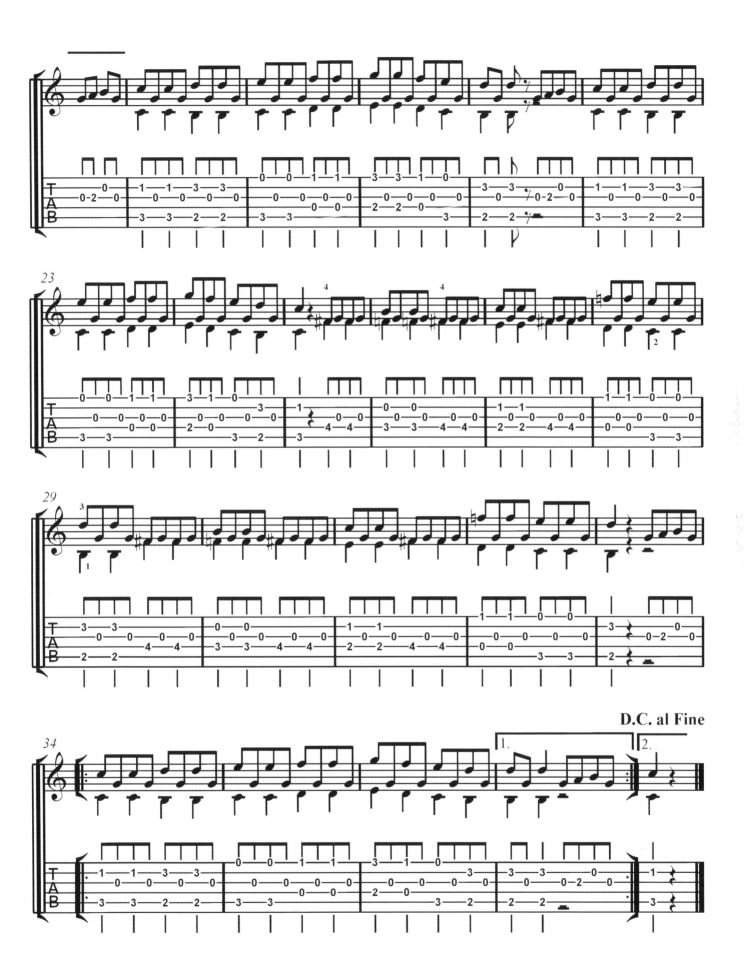

D.C. al Fine

15. Scarborough Fair (Traditional)

Scarborough Fair is one of the most well-known folk songs ever written. Much of its enduring appeal is due to the folk revival of the 1960s. Paul Simon learnt the song from renowned English folk guitarist Martin Carthy, and Simon & Garfunkel recorded it in 1968.

Like most folk songs and stories, Scarborough Fair has many variations. Our arrangement consists of a short introduction, followed by two repeats of the melody, then a repeat of the introduction to finish. Several different textures are used to keep the piece interesting. In each section, observe how many notes are struck simultaneously, and whether chords change once per bar, or if a new chord is on every note of the tune.

The opening combines fretted notes higher up the neck with open strings. Shapes like these produce interesting intervals by allowing notes that are close together to ring out simultaneously. This texture is evocative of Celtic harp playing.

Bars five to eight contain the first phrase of the tune. The melody is played using notes found in common open chords. In bar seven, the C Major chord should be held down for the whole bar, with only your first finger being removed to play the F note.

The next phrase pairs the melody notes with a harmony a sixth below. The open string bass notes should be allowed to ring out. Be careful with the arching of your fingers to avoid muting them accidentally, especially in bar eleven where the open string is between the two fretted notes.

Bars seventeen to twenty employ tenth-intervals, as seen in several previous pieces, such as Carulli's Andantino. The melody will sound smoothest if you avoid using the same finger consecutively when transitioning between notes.

Another harp-inspired moment occurs in bars twenty-three and twenty-four. The melody notes E, C, F and D all ring together, creating a chord known as a cluster.

Treat both pairs of notes in bar twenty-five like a chord shape, so they ring together, giving a thicker sound. Keep your first finger on the high E-string, then use your fourth finger for the chord in bar twenty-six to preserve the momentum.

Follow the fingering in bar thirty-three carefully to make the position shift smooth. The open C chord in the previous bar means you're starting on your third finger. The whole of bar thirty-three uses just fingers two and three. Keep the third finger on the B-string into the next bar.

Once you are able to play the piece at a steady tempo, add some expressive phrasing. A great way to decide where and how this should be done is to sing the song out loud, or listen to it sung (preferably unaccompanied). Note the points in the tune where there is rise or fall in volume, and how the tempo slows down towards the end of each phrase. Replicating these nuances will add a lot to your performance and can make seemingly simple music captivating.

Scarborough Fair (Traditional)

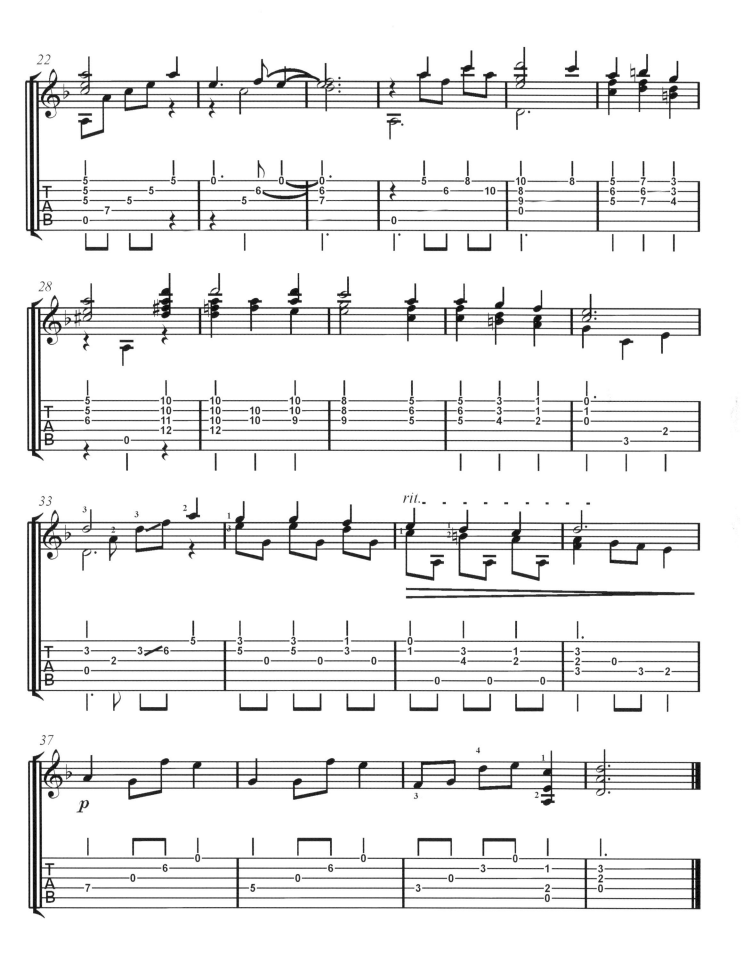

16. Op.4, Bagatelle No. 10 – Heinrich Marschner

Although less well remembered than his contemporaries (Beethoven, Wagner and Schumann), Heinrich Marschner was a master of German opera and much adored during his lifetime. He also wrote songs and instrumental chamber music.

One of his early published works is a collection of twelve bagatelles, published in Leipzig in 1812. Bagatelles are short, light pieces without any presupposed mood or structure.

A steady semiquaver pattern is maintained for much of the piece. However, the placement of the notes changes, so the challenge is to vary the fingerpicking patterns without losing speed. In the first two sections a single melody note is played with your M or A fingers, while your P and I fingers (or P, I and M in bar three) are on the off-beats.

The third section reverses the pattern. Here the bassline and melody note are together on the beat, with the open G string providing an answering pedal tone throughout. This requires pinching P and M on the beats, with I plucking the G in the gaps.

In bar twelve, I've broken down the best left-hand fingering for the descending double-stop line. The repeated high Gs in the previous bar should be held down with your fourth finger, and the diminished chord on beat 2 played with your other three fingers. Then there is a quick position shift for the double-stop.

In bars thirteen and fourteen the pedal tone is paired with smaller, but equally sweet-sounding sixth intervals. The familiar tenth intervals then make a return in bar fifteen.

Once all the notes are in place and you're performing the piece at a steady tempo, you can look at the subtle details in the piece.

All the off-beat chords in the first half of the piece should be short and detached, as indicated by the semiquaver rests. This gives a greater sense of contrast between the melody and chords.

To control the length of the notes, practise bringing your thumb and first finger to rest on their strings immediately after plucking them, keeping the other fingers well out of the way, so you're not stifling the melody.

Op.4 Bagatelle No. 10 - Heinrich Marschner

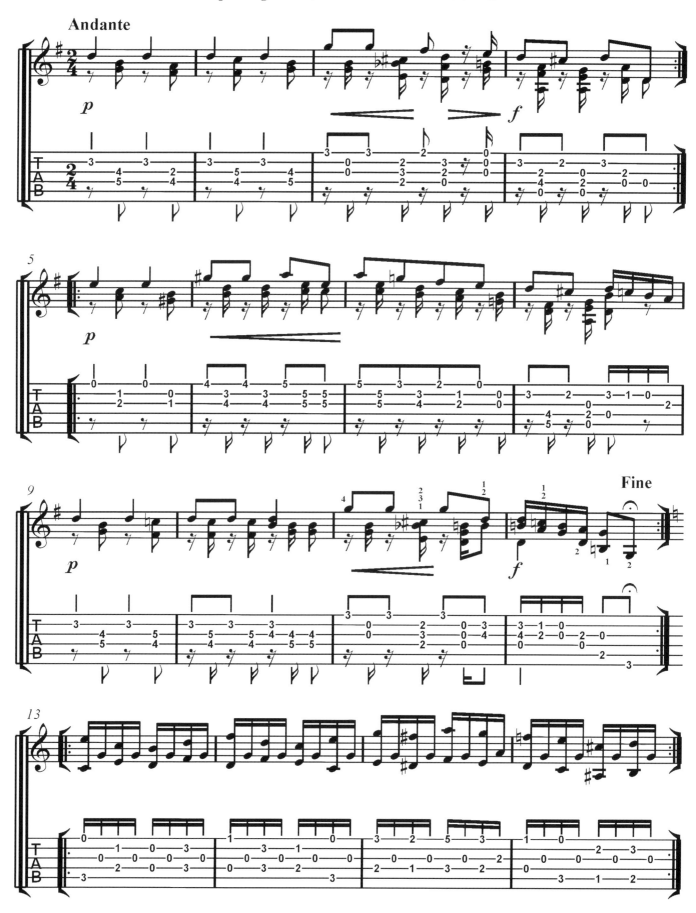

17. Op. 10, No. 1 – Matteo Carcassi

Now we return to the music of Carcassi to explore his Opus 10 collection, entitled *Twelve Easy Pieces.*

The speed indicated in the score is *allegretto non troppo*, which means walking pace, but without being fast. The target tempo for performing the piece is 105 bpm. You should spend plenty of time playing each section at a slower tempo.

The combination of thumb and finger interplay, and bursts of single notes, will develop the picking hand.

Use your thumb when there are tails below the tab and notation. Everything else should be plucked with your fingers. Your thumb's different tone and attack will help separate the bassline from the other notes.

Make use of your fourth finger to fret several of the melody notes, as this will allow you to keep the bass notes held down for longer. In bar one, the low C and G should be played with your third finger (as in a common open C chord), so the fourth finger can catch the melody notes at the 3rd fret in the first two bars.

In bar three, use fingers one and two for the first chord, and your fourth finger for the D on beat 2. This leaves your fourth finger available to make a smooth transition to the next bass note at the 3rd fret.

A particularly difficult section is the single-note run in bar sixteen. The picking pattern breaks down here and to get the necessary speed, your picking hand should alternate between two plucking fingers (I and M) on a single string. To get a more consistent attack, it may help to reposition the hand slightly to present the two fingers to the string more equally, rather than on a slant.

On a technical level, the first twelve bars will feel like playing slow sustained notes with your thumb, while maintaining an alternating figure with your fingers. On a musical level, it can be seen as a bassline and a crotchet melody line moving in counterpoint, while a third layer of open Gs slots in between. The notes on the beats can be played slightly louder than the Gs to bring out the tune, but this requires a high level of control.

Op. 10, No. 1 – Matteo Carcassi

Allegretto non troppo

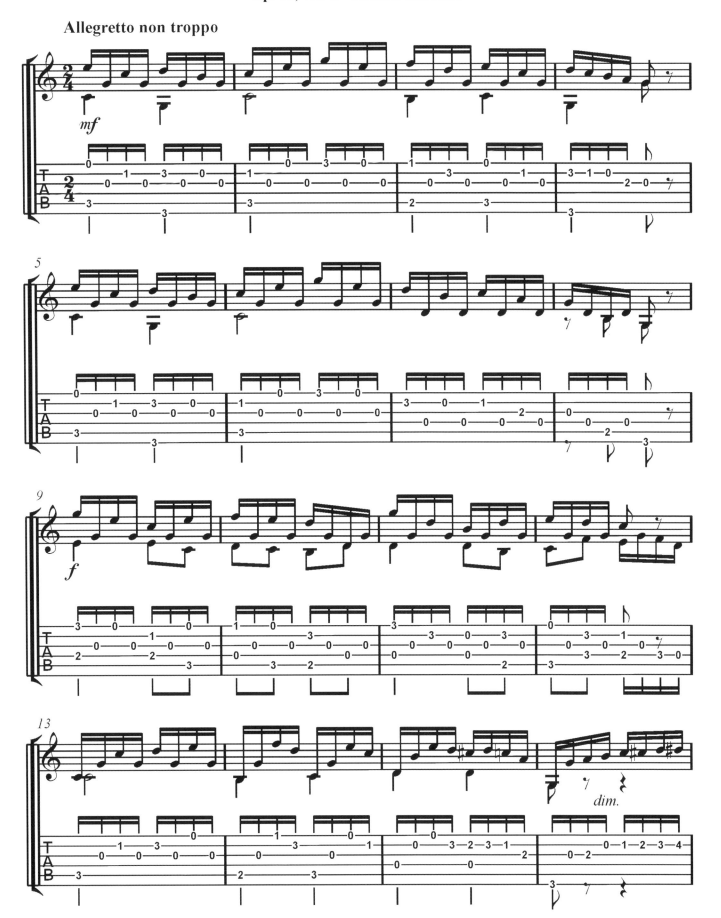

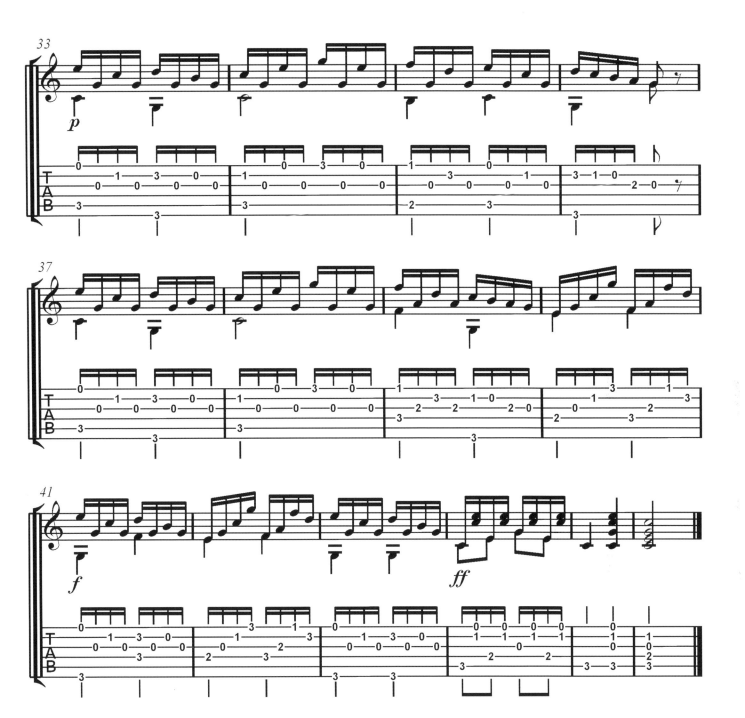

18. Lágrima – Francisco Tárrega

Tárrega's beautiful *Lágrima* (Teardrop) is typical of the Spanish Romantic style. The composer manages to make the usually bright, sunny key of E Major drip with wistful nostalgia. After the main theme, the music switches to the parallel key of E Minor, producing an even darker mood.

Parallel modulations like the one in Lágrima make the destination minor key feel even sadder.

Keep your fourth finger held down for the sequence of tenths in bar one. The bottom note in each pair should be fretted with either your first or second finger, depending on whether it is a one-fret or two-fret span.

To allow bars two and four to ring out properly, start with your first and fourth fingers (continuing from the previous bar), then add the third and second fingers as they're needed. Keep your fingers arched to make sure you aren't accidentally muting any notes. The chord should "swell" over the course of the bar as more notes are added.

Bar five will take a bit more preparation. Be sure to bar the top four strings straight away so that the B on the D-string will be ready when the time comes.

After your second finger moves up to the 11th fret in bar six, your remaining fingers should form an A Minor chord shape underneath it (the shape will look like A Minor, but because of the position, is F#m).

On beat 2 of bar seven you should again pre-emptively barre right across the 2nd fret, so that the following bass note is already held down. This will avoid repositioning mid-phrase.

From bar nine there are several position shifts that need to be well practised to execute well. The first shift features an expressive slide, which builds the energy by exaggerating the rise in pitch. The C at the 8th fret should be re-picked after you slide up to it. This is rhythmically tricky, so listen carefully to the audio.

Thankfully, there are open string notes before most of the position shifts. It might take time to develop your hand independence, but aim to make the leap as the picking hand plays the open strings, without letting the tempo falter.

Lágrima – Francisco Tárrega

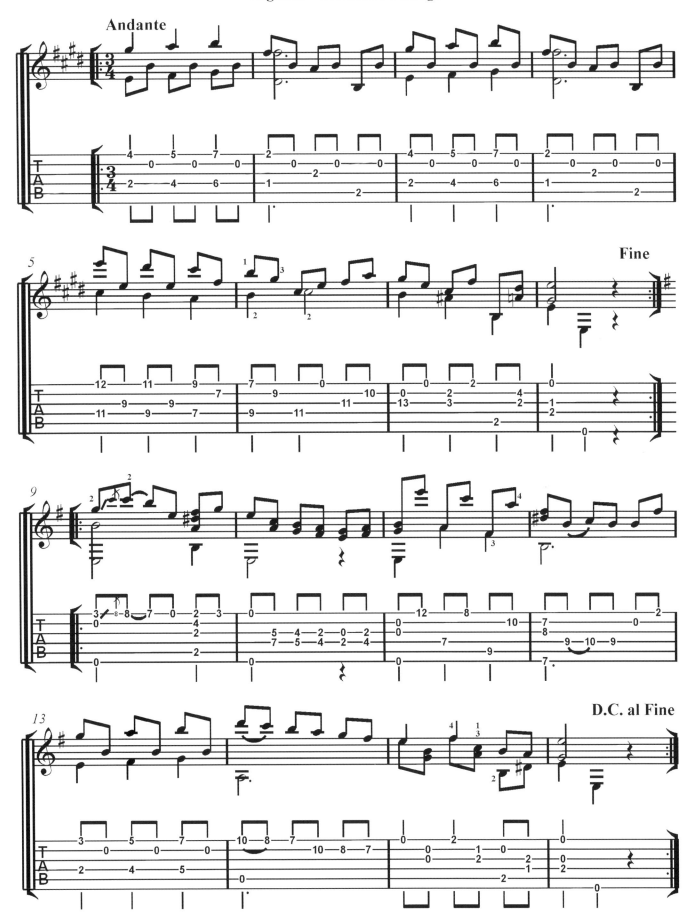

19. Bourrée in E Minor – J.S. Bach

A *bourrée* is a French dance, though it was popular throughout Western European society during Bach's lifetime (1685-1750). The guitar did exist at this time, in roughly its modern form, but was still mainly limited to Spain, so Bach, being German, would have been more familiar with the lute.

Bach was employed primarily as a church organist. His repertoire was mainly religious choral works and instrumental keyboard music.

This much-loved piece is from a larger suite containing six movements. Each movement is based on different dance forms. The piece wouldn't have been intended to be danced to, but adopts the musical characteristics of a *bourrée* as a starting point.

The Bourrée in E Minor is a perfect example of counterpoint: two simultaneous melodies that are independent, but at the same time complementary.

Within counterpoint there are two ways the melodies can interact. Moving in similar motion (both voices going up or down in pitch together) or *contrary motion* (going in opposite directions). Look at the first four bars of the notation and see how the two lines of dots "concertina" towards and away from each other. This melodic shape is an example of contrary motion.

When listening to the audio, focus on either the higher or lower voice and follow it from start to finish. This skill of "editorial" listening will improve with practise, and will allow you to hear all sorts of details in music.

Bourrée in E Minor – J.S. Bach

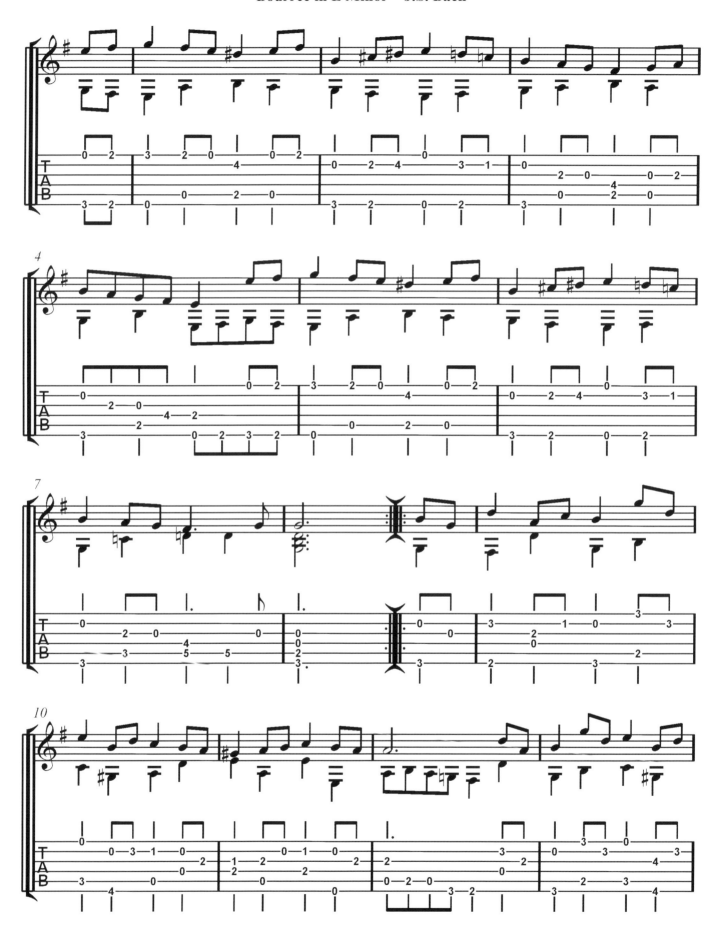

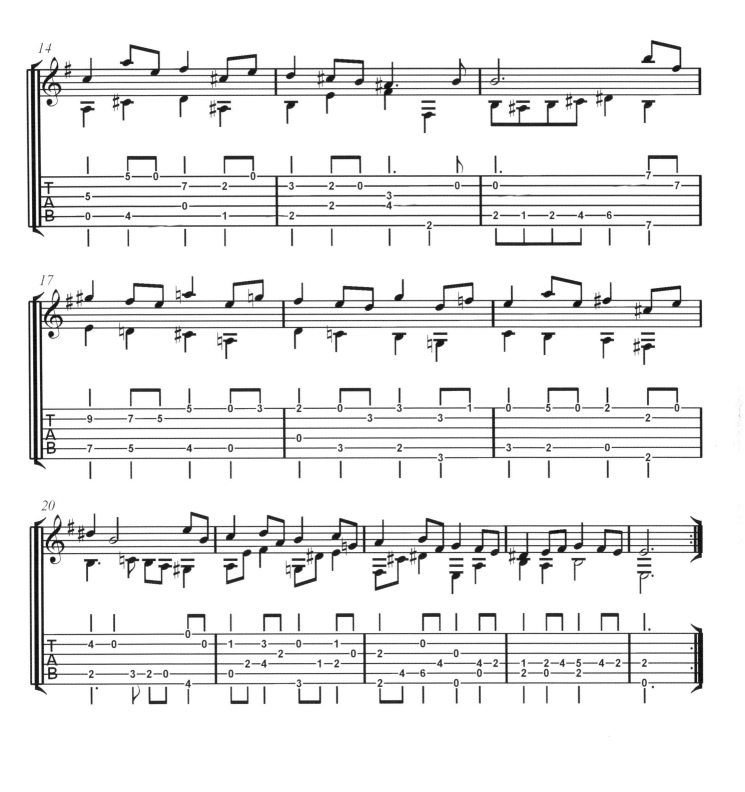

20. Op. 35, Study No. 22 – Fernando Sor

Most of the classical studies examined so far have focused on developing your picking hand. In Sor's Study No. 22 (one of his most widely played and enduringly popular solo pieces), the picking hand can settle into a repetitive pattern while you focus on your fretting hand's strength and stamina.

There are several instances of full barre chords in Study No. 22. Many players find it difficult to maintain barres for any length of time and to move smoothly between them. Other chords use open strings alongside fretted notes, so the fingers must be arched and positioned accurately in order to let everything ring out properly.

The key to a reliable barre technique is to make the most efficient contact with the instrument. Start by placing your first finger across the 2nd fret for the opening B Minor chord. It should be as close to the metal as possible, with the fret almost under the finger. Keep your thumb straight in the middle of the neck, as if giving a thumb print.

Don't stack your remaining fingers on top of your first finger to press it down. Each finger should be independent and the barre must be unsupported, so your other fingers are free to form the rest of the chord.

There are three different instances of barres in this piece and only the F# Major chord in bar thirty-two, and F#7 in bar forty-seven, require all six strings.

There are some subtle fingering choices that will help you make the chord changes as smooth as possible. In bar three, use your first and third fingers. Practise swapping strings with the first finger from bar two to bar three, while letting the previous notes ring out for as long as possible.

In bars four to six, keep the first finger on the B-string to give you a fixed point of reference, while your second and third fingers swap strings.

Start by tackling the piece as a chord study. Identify each shape and make sure the changes are smooth as possible, with no buzzing on the barre chords.

I've simplified the notation compared to how Sor wrote it. All the notes are in the correct place, but he made stricter demands on how long each note should be. The extra note tails gave the piece a confusing appearance on the page but allowed the music to be clearly seen as a series of layered melodic lines.

The rest-stroke technique, seen in Tárrega's Study in E Minor (page 41), would also work well here to accentuate the highest notes once the chord shapes have been mastered.

Listen to some recordings by masterful guitarists such as Julian Bream or Andrés Segovia, and you can appreciate how the highest notes in each bar are accented to bring out the lilting melody.

Op. 35, Study No. 22 – Fernando Sor

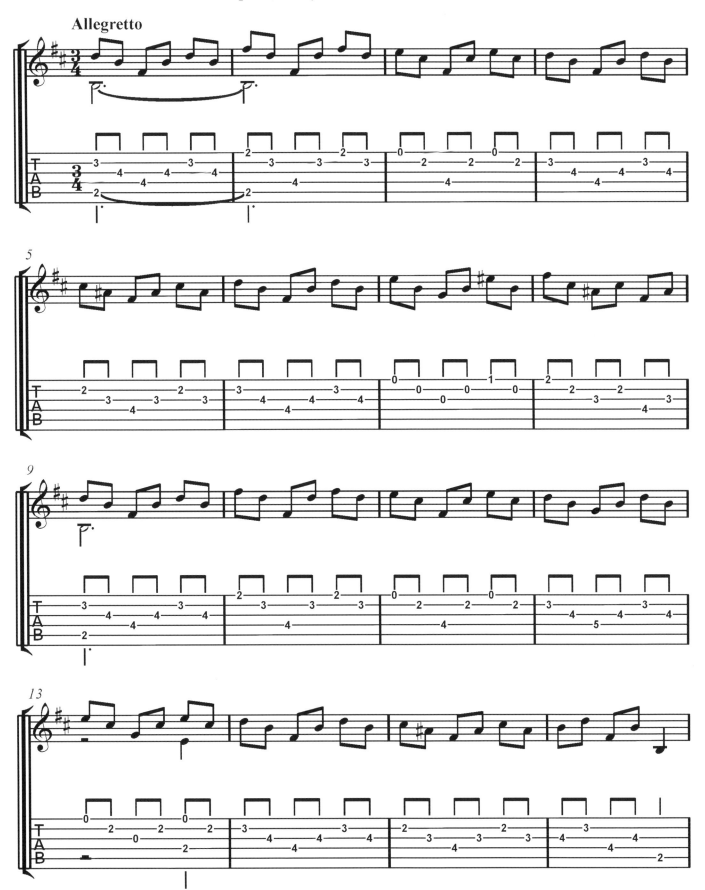

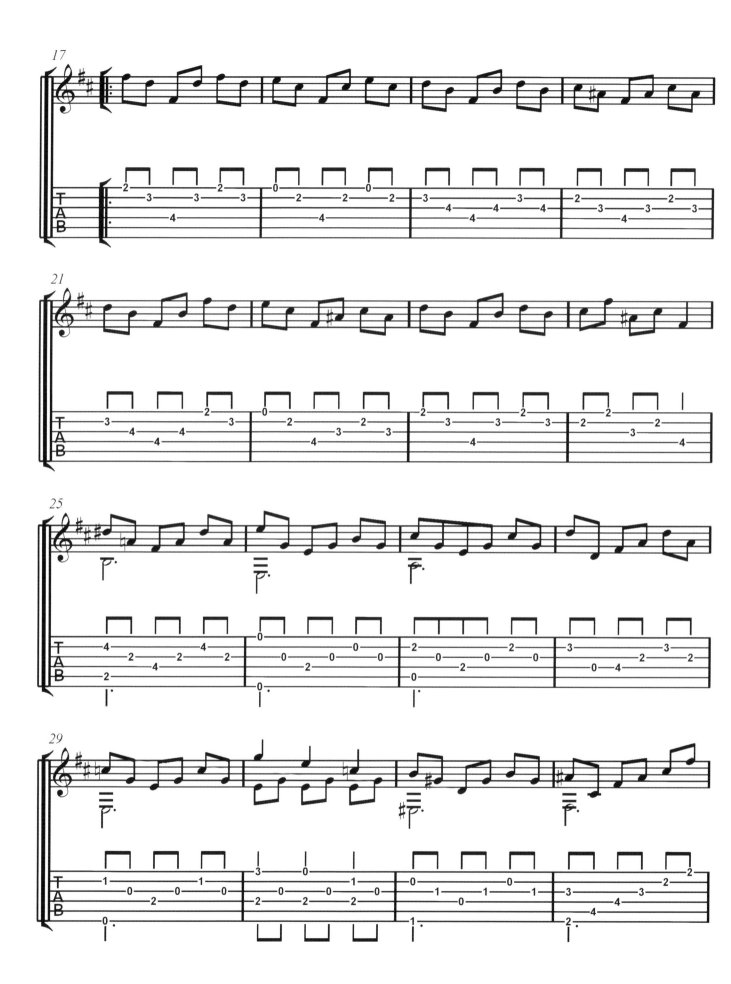

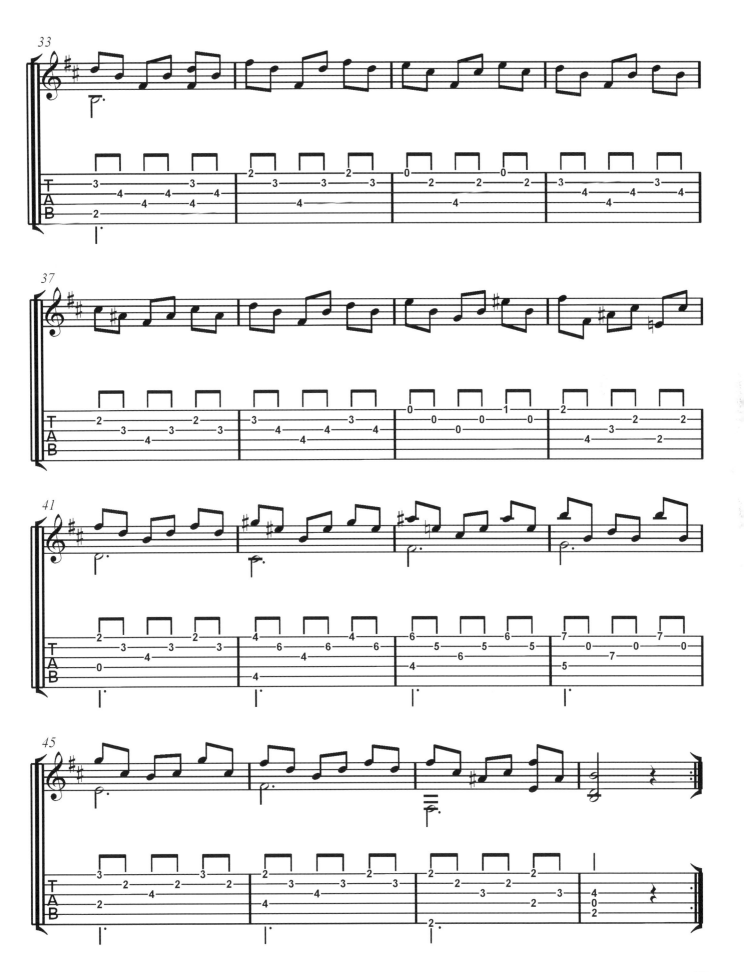

Closing Words

I hope you've enjoyed working through the pieces. Being able to perform full pieces is the most rewarding part of learning an instrument. It's the payoff for all the effort put into studying technique and theory.

I encourage you to explore other works by the composers you've most enjoyed. It's important to listen widely and critically to help you discern the nuances of great players, and train your ear to hear subtle details in the music.

These works were selected so that the technical level of the book developed gradually while remaining approachable to the beginner, the skills that you've built here will allow you to unlock more challenging pieces in future.

I encourage you to explore other works by the composers you've most enjoyed.

I included music from different periods, such as Baroque, Classical and Romantic, as well as some folk-inspired pieces too. It is interesting to hear the similarities in pieces from each era, as well as how guitar playing has developed over four centuries.

Listen to the audio that accompanies each piece in this book, but also seek out other recordings of the tunes and listen to how each guitarist approaches the music. Listen for variations in tempo, and changes in volume and speed. Hearing multiple performances will illustrate different approaches and help you create your own interpretations.

Other Books from Fundamental Changes

The Complete Guide to Playing Blues Guitar Book One: Rhythm Guitar

The Complete Guide to Playing Blues Guitar Book Two: Melodic Phrasing

The Complete Guide to Playing Blues Guitar Book Three: Beyond Pentatonics

The Complete Guide to Playing Blues Guitar Compilation

The CAGED System and 100 Licks for Blues Guitar

Minor ii V Mastery for Jazz Guitar

Jazz Blues Soloing for Guitar

Guitar Scales in Context

Guitar Chords in Context

The First 100 Chords for Guitar

Jazz Guitar Chord Mastery

Complete Technique for Modern Guitar

Funk Guitar Mastery

The Complete Technique, Theory & Scales Compilation for Guitar

Sight Reading Mastery for Guitar

Rock Guitar Un-CAGED

The Practical Guide to Modern Music Theory for Guitarists

Beginner's Guitar Lessons: The Essential Guide

Chord Tone Soloing for Jazz Guitar

Chord Tone Soloing for Bass Guitar

Voice Leading Jazz Guitar

Guitar Fretboard Fluency

The Circle of Fifths for Guitarists

First Chord Progressions for Guitar

The First 100 Jazz Chords for Guitar

100 Country Licks for Guitar

Pop & Rock Ukulele Strumming

Walking Bass for Jazz and Blues

Guitar Finger Gym

The Melodic Minor Cookbook

The Chicago Blues Guitar Method

Heavy Metal Rhythm Guitar

Heavy Metal Lead Guitar

Progressive Metal Guitar

Heavy Metal Guitar Bible

Exotic Pentatonic Soloing for Guitar

The Complete Jazz Guitar Soloing Compilation

The Jazz Guitar Chords Compilation

Fingerstyle Blues Guitar

The Complete DADGAD Guitar Method

Country Guitar for Beginners

Beginner Lead Guitar Method

The Country Fingerstyle Guitar Method

Beyond Rhythm Guitar

Rock Rhythm Guitar Playing

Fundamental Changes in Jazz Guitar

Neo-Classical Speed Strategies for Guitar

100 Classic Rock Licks for Guitar

The Beginner's Guitar Method Compilation

100 Classic Blues Licks for Guitar

The Country Guitar Method Compilation

Country Guitar Soloing Techniques

Printed in Poland
by Amazon Fulfillment
Poland Sp. z o.o., Wrocław